THE
POCKET BOOK
OF
ASTON VILLA

By Dave Woodhall

Published by Vision Sports Publishing in 2010

Vision Sports Publishing
19-23 High Street
Kingston upon Thames
Surrey
KT1 1LL

www.visionsp.co.uk

Text © Dave Woodhall
Illustrations © Bob Bond Sporting Caricatures

ISBN: 978-1905326-95-2

Series editor: Jim Drewett
Series production: Martin Cloake
Design: Neal Cobourne
Illustrations: Bob Bond
Cover photography: Paul Downes, Objective Image
All pictures: Getty Images unless otherwise stated
Thanks to Greg Upton and Stewart Lindsay

Printed and bound in China by Toppan Printing Co Ltd

A CIP catalogue record for this book is available from the British Library

THIS IS AN UNOFFICIAL PUBLICATION

All statistics in *The Pocket Book of Aston Villa* are correct up until the end
of the 2009/10 season.

CONTENTS

FOREWORD BY
GARY SHAW

When I was a youngster growing up in Birmingham during the 1970s I used to go down the Villa religiously. Standing on the Holte End I would watch my heroes, great players such as Andy Lochhead, Ray Graydon and Brian Little, my favourite. Like every other lad in the crowd I would dream of putting on that world-famous claret and blue shirt and playing for the Villa. But for me the dream came true. Not only that, I went on to replace my hero, Brian Little, in the team.

I'll never forget the first time I ran out onto the pitch, with a packed Holte End watching me in the same way I used to watch my idols. As far as I'm aware none of the Villa players who came after me were there when I made my debut, but you never know...

Even now I find it hard to believe just what that wonderful team of which I was a part managed to achieve in such a short time. League champions, European champions, European Super Cup winners. What we did in those few years was a magnificent achievement and I wonder how much more we could have done had circumstances been different. We had great players and in Ron Saunders and the often-overlooked Tony Barton we had great managers.

But whatever happened in the past, and may happen in the future, there is still something about Aston Villa that means much more than just their triumphs on the pitch. From the great Victorian era to the present day, the history of our club is rich in stories, legends and mystique. This book picks out some of the best, the most unusual and some of the lesser-known events that deserve to be remembered. I've enjoyed reading them and I'm sure you will, too.

Since my playing days there have been good times and bad. Villa have once more got plenty to look forward to under the impressive ownership of Randy Lerner and I'm certain there will be much more success to come. The faces may have changed but I still get the same buzz of excitement when I'm working at Villa Park on a match day as I always did and sometimes I wonder if there are any more young lads in the crowd who are going to come off the Holte End to take their place in the team. I hope so.

...CLUB DIRECTORY...

Club address: Villa Park, Aston,
           Birmingham, B6 6HE
Club reception: 0121 327 2299
Club website: www.avfc.co.uk
Ticket and merchandise sales:
           0800 612 0970
Online merchandise sales:
           www.astonvilladirect.com
           Hospitality and events:
           0800 612 0960
           www.avhe.co.uk
           Holte Hotel: 0800 612 0940

LEIGHTON PHILLIPS
ASTON VILLA

Junior Supporters Club:

       www.avlife.co.uk

Aston Villa Disabled Supporters
Association: www.avids.co.uk

Aston Villa Supporters Trust:

       www.villatrust.org.uk

Aston Villa Former Players Association:

       www.astonvillafpa.org

Supporters clubs: www.avfclionsclubs.co.uk

Official club charity: www.acorns.org.uk

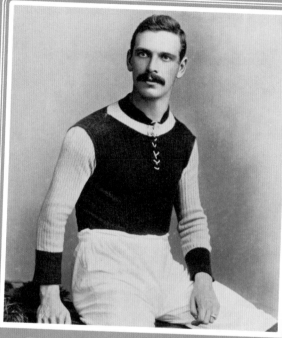

THE STORY OF THE VILLA
THE EARLY DAYS
1874-1914

The exact story behind the formation of Aston Villa is lost in the mists of time. It is generally accepted that four members of the Aston Villa cricket club met under a lamppost in Heathfield Rd, part of what is now the suburb of Lozells in the city of Birmingham, one evening towards the end of 1874 to discuss ways of keeping fit during the winter.

One theory has it that they originally wanted to play rugby, but were dissuaded after watching a particularly brutal game which took place nearby.

Ironically, when they did form a football club their first game, against Aston Brook St Mary's in March 1875, was a 15-a-side affair with the first half played to rugby rules and the second association football. The game was scoreless at half time and Villa

Legend has it that the club was formed at a meeting under a suburban lamppost

eventually won 1-0, thanks to a goal scored by Jack
Hughes with a ball hired for the occasion at the cost
of one shilling.

Villa's first FA Cup-
winning team pose with
the trophy in 1887

For the first few years of their existence Villa
were similar to many other local teams, living a
nomadic existence and playing most of their games
on Aston Park. However the arrival in Birmingham
of Scotsmen George Ramsay and Archie Hunter
was to herald an upswing in the club's fortunes.
Hunter was the first great player the Villa fielded,
while Ramsay proved himself to be one of the finest
administrators the game has ever known. He ran
the club in conjunction with other visionaries such
as William McGregor on proper business lines and
found the Villa's first permanent home at Wellington
Rd, Perry Barr.

The great Double-winning team of 1896/97

Villa had by now established themselves as the pre-eminent club in Birmingham and won their first major trophy, the FA Cup, in 1887 by beating local rivals West Bromwich Albion 2-0 at the Oval. They then, however, entered a period of comparative decline which resulted in a bitter argument between club members in 1892 and the arrival on the scene of the third of the triumvirate of Villa administrators, Frederick Rinder. With men of such ability running

the club it was no surprise that Villa went on to establish the first great dynasty in English football.

The league championship was won five times in seven seasons between 1894 and 1900, and the FA Cup twice. In 1896/97 Villa became the second side to complete the double, winning the cup by beating Everton 3-2 in a game reckoned to be the finest played in the 19th century.

The Villa side of this era included such great names as Charlie Athersmith, hailed as the finest winger in the world at the time, captain John Devey and Howard Spencer, the 'Prince of Full Backs'. Not only were the team setting new standards on the field, off the pitch the club were just as innovative. Villa committee member William McGregor had been the inspiration behind the formation of the Football League and he, together with the rest of the Villa board, were now turning their business acumen towards what was at the time the most forward-thinking football club in the world. They were the first to cultivate a youth policy based on signing youngsters from local sides rather than established players (although this did not stop them from regularly breaking the world transfer record), to adapt their tactics according to the opposition in a particular game and also to organise travel for supporters to away fixtures.

Such was the Villa's hold on the imagination of the sporting public that stories about the club entered popular folklore. The theft of the FA Cup in 1895 was one of the more embarrassing tales, while the tale of Charlie Athersmith holding an umbrella while playing during a thunderstorm was one of the more unlikely. There were also several examples of Villa

Harry Hampton, centre, scores after two minutes in the 1905 FA Cup final against Newcastle at Crystal Palace

playing benefit matches in aid of cash-strapped local clubs such as Small Heath Alliance and Walsall. The club obviously remembered its roots in the 'muscular Christianity' that was prevalent during the reign of Queen Victoria.

By now the old ground at Wellington Road was woefully inadequate for the finest football team in the world and a new one capable of holding 50,000 was built on the site of the Aston Lower Grounds, adjacent to the club's former headquarters at Aston Park. This opened in April 1897, the month in which the double was won, and was the finest in the country.

The new capacity was soon tested. Villa's attendances were the highest in the league and the club continued

Tossing up at Ewood Park before the 1912/13 FA Cup semifinal against Oldham

to amass trophies and set new standards.

Some of the old stagers continued to shine and they were joined by other names such as 'Happy' Harry Hampton, often regarded as Villa's finest centre forward of all time. The club's form slipped slightly during the first decade of the 20th century, although they won the FA Cup for a fourth time in 1905 and followed this up five years later with their sixth league championship. Little did supporters know as they celebrated this particular triumph that it would be another 71 years before the famous trophy returned to Villa Park. They also finished runners-up the following season.

A fifth FA Cup win came in 1913, against Sunderland, and another first for the Villa as the final was the first to take place in the presence of royalty. The cup was presented to Villa captain Joe Bache by the Earl of Plymouth. Villa finished runners-up in the league in both 1912/13 and the following season, narrowly failing to emulate the double triumph of 1897 on both occasions. By now the club's star players included Sam Hardy, reckoned the best goalkeeper in the Villa's history, and Clem Stephenson, who later went on to win three league championships with Huddersfield Town. But the shadow of war was falling across Europe and when hostilities finally broke out in August 1914 not only did they bring with them the shattering of the old order but also the end of one of the greatest eras of success any football club has ever enjoyed.

BADGE OF HONOUR

Villa were the first club in England to have the Scottish lion rampant as their badge, one of many innovations made during the Victorian era. It is believed that director William McGregor, a proud Scotsman, was responsible – as he was for many of the club's groundbreaking achievements. Many have since copied, but yet again it was Aston Villa they were imitating.

Johnny Dixon smooches the FA Cup in the first season Villa shirts sported a badge

It's reckoned that for a time in the early days the team played in colours which featured a large lion rampant. However, this practice was soon discontinued, although a photograph of the 1887 FA Cup-winning side shows several of them wearing shirts bearing the Birmingham civic crest.

The official club badge comprised of a lion rampant inside a curved shield and the club motto 'Prepared' in a scroll underneath. This badge featured prominently around Villa Park, most notably above the magnificent staircase which formed the centrepiece of the Trinity Road stand, but was not a feature of the playing kit until several decades later.

The badge was finally added to the players' shirts for the 1956/57 season, just in time to be shown as Johnny Dixon lifted the FA Cup at Wembley. Claret

against a blue background, this remained the instantly-recognisable emblem of the club until 1969, when the revolution led by Doug Ellis and Tommy Docherty meant changes were afoot in the world of Aston Villa. Tradition was cast aside in favour of modernity as both playing kit and badge were altered. The image of the lion rampant remained on the shirt but was now blue and no longer surrounded by a shield, and the letters 'A.V.' were now displayed underneath.

Brian Little wearing the 1969 modernist design

The summer of 1974 saw several more significant changes. Ron Saunders became manager and the Villa's most obvious public symbols were once more modernised. The kit was altered slightly while the club badge was changed to the most iconic design of modern times – the familiar claret lion on a blue background but now inside a circular shield, with the words 'Aston Villa FC' picked out in gold

The badge Villa wore as they reclaimed their place at football's summit in the 1970s

around the perimeter. This was the image which was to become famous as Villa first re-established themselves as a major force in English football and then went on to conquer Europe.

However, the new badge was not greeted with unanimous approval. Veteran club stalwart Eric Houghton, by now a member of the board, claimed that the lettering was yellow, which he said was "a coward's colour".

Gordon Cowans in the club's 1978 glory days

This badge remained throughout the most successful period in the Villa's post-war history, up until the summer of 1992. The brave new world of the Premier League meant that once more the old was being cast aside and Villa yet again had a new kit (although this news was becoming less a novelty than an annual event) with a new badge to go with it.

The revamped design saw the shape of the shield altered with the introduction of straight lines, the lion rampart was now gold on a claret and blue striped background for some reason, with the words 'Aston Villa FC' above and the club motto 'Prepared' below.

The badge was slightly altered over the years, with Villa director Mark Ansell saying at one point that the lion had begun to look more like a seahorse, and

it was noted at one point that the letters 'FC' were removed just as the sport itself was becoming less important than the related business interests it presented.

'FC' eventually reappeared but the next major change came with the club's new ownership.

Randy Lerner's takeover meant that the Villa were once more moving in a fresh direction and needed a new badge to represent these changes. The design which was revealed in the summer of 2007 has remained unaltered ever since. It retains the shield from the 1992 version and contains a golden lion on a light blue background. The legends 'AVFC' and 'Prepared' are prominent inside the shield, as is a silver star to denote the club's winning of the European Cup in 1982. In line with the openness of the current owners, certain elements of the badge came about as a result of an online poll amongst supporters.

As the badge evolved in the 1990s, the lion seemed to some to be morphing into a seahorse

The latest badge, clean and simple with a star to mark the 1982 European Cup win

1982 AND ALL THAT

Villa were unlikely winners of the 1980/81 First Division title and, with the national press having ignored them for most of the season, it was only natural that the team's chances of adding the European Cup to their list of successes should also be written off.

The team eased their way into the competition with a 5-0 win at home against Icelandic champions Valur, with reserve striker Terry Donovan creating a small piece of history by scoring Villa's first goal. This was then followed by a straightforward 2-0 victory in the away leg, of which the most abiding memory for the hardy band of Villa supporters who made the journey was the revolting smell emanating from a nearby fish processing plant.

So far so simple, but the second round provided

a much stiffer test in the shape of East German side
Dinamo Berlin. Dinamo were the side of the Stasi secret
police, hated by the population of the city but on their
way to ten consecutive league championships thanks
to bribery of referees and being able to acquire the star
names of their rivals. Villa's performance in Berlin was
their best of the competition, Jimmy Rimmer saving a
penalty and Tony Morley scoring one of the finest goals
of his career after running almost the length of the
pitch with the ball. Villa won the first leg 2-1 and were
grateful of the lead after a poor display in the Villa Park
return saw them go down 1-0 on the night and proceed
nervously to the next round on away goals.

In between the defeat of Dinamo Berlin and
the quarter-finals, Villa were rocked by the
shock resignation of manager Ron Saunders.
His replacement, initially on a temporary basis,
was assistant Tony Barton. The venue for the
away leg was also in dispute for some time.
Dynamo Kiev of the USSR were to be Villa's
opponents but with the game taking place in
March, Dynamo would be unable to play at
their own frozen ground. After some wrangling
the tie was scheduled for the Crimean city of
Simferopol. There Villa had to overcome what
could be diplomatically described as many
'cultural differences' to gain a creditable 0-0
draw against a side which featured the bulk
of the Russian national side, including former
European Footballer of the Year Oleg Blokhin.

The second leg at Villa Park was expected to be tough but goals from Gary Shaw and Ken McNaught saw Villa ease through and into a semi-final date with Belgian side Anderlecht.

By the time of the semi Barton had been made team manager on a permanent basis. Villa's opponents may not have been particularly well-known but they had a useful record in Europe and would go on to win the following season's UEFA Cup. Manager Tomislav Ivic was infamous for his defensive tactics and another fine individual goal from Tony Morley proved decisive. Against a backdrop of violence on the terraces, and a solo pitch invader, Villa gave a thoroughly professional performance to keep the return leg goalless and so go through to the European Cup final in their first season in the competition. However, before they could make any further plans they had to endure a UEFA inquiry into the disturbances surrounding the away leg of the semi.

Anderlecht had called for Villa's expulsion but the Villa defence team, led by former Minister of Sport and local MP Denis Howell, successfully argued against this move. The club were, though, ordered to play their next home tie behind closed doors.

And so on to the de Kuip stadium in Rotterdam to play legendary German side Bayern Munich, three times winners of the competition and taking part in their 13th major final, having never previously lost one. The scene was set for a memorable night, and so it proved. Veteran goalkeeper Jimmy Rimmer was forced to leave the field after nine minutes, to be replaced by rookie Nigel Spink in only his second senior game. Spink pulled off a string of magnificent saves as the Germans began to dominate the game and when he was finally beaten, Kenny Swain was on hand to head off the line.

Then came the move which started in midfield and ended up with Peter Withe scoring the only goal of the match. Unfancied Villa, with a manager who had only been in the job a matter of weeks, had become European Champions just ten years after playing in the Third Division. The European Cup stayed in England for a sixth consecutive year and a host of media experts had to admit that they had been wrong in writing off Villa's chances of winning the biggest prize in club football. Sorry, my mistake. That was one thing not even the all-conquering Villa side could achieve.

ASTON VILLA

COMIC STRIP HISTORY

1

THE 1977 LEAGUE CUP FINAL BETWEEN VILLA AND EVERTON WAS ONE OF THE DULLEST IN HISTORY, FINISHING GOALLESS. THE REPLAY WAS NOT MUCH BETTER ...

I'VE SPENT BETTER AFTERNOONS AT THE DENTIST...

EVERTON WERE 1-0 UP IN THE SECOND REPLAY AT OLD TRAFFORD WHEN VILLA CAPTAIN CHRIS NICHOLL LET FLY FROM 40 YARDS. IT SCREAMED INTO THE NET !

WITHIN MINUTES BRIAN LITTLE PUT VILLA 2-1 AHEAD ...

...ONLY FOR EVERTON TO EQUALISE ALMOST IMMEDIATELY...2-2 !

THERE WERE ONLY SECONDS LEFT IN EXTRA-TIME WHEN LITTLE SCORED VILLA'S WINNER — AFTER 330 MINUTES, PLUS INJURY TIME.

THE FIRST TWO GAMES MAY HAVE BEEN BORING, BUT THE SECOND REPLAY WAS THE MOST EXCITING LEAGUE CUP FINAL OF ALL TIME ...

VILLA PARK

By 1897 the greatest football club in the world needed a new ground. Not only was their Wellington Road headquarters inadequate for the crowds they were attracting, but the landlord, mindful of the club's popularity, was charging them ever-increasing rent. A site was found on the old Aston Lower Grounds, a part of Aston Park where the club had played in their early days, and work commenced on what was to become the most modern football ground in the land.

A colour illustration of Villa Park as it was in 1900

Villa Park, as it soon became known, opened on 17th April 1897 with a game against Blackburn Rovers. It attracted 15,000 spectators who braved torrential rain to witness Villa win 3-0. Two days later a crowd of 50,000 set a Football League record attendance as

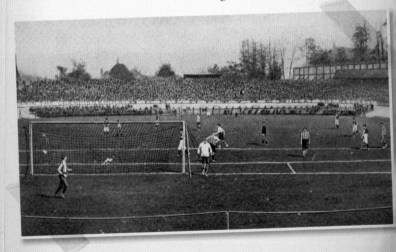

Villa beat Wolves 5-0, although the day was marred by a fatal accident during a cycle race which took place before the game.

At this time Villa Park's capacity was reckoned to be 70,000 and, after the club purchased the freehold of the ground from Flowers brewery in 1911, plans were put into place to extend it to 130,000. Unfortunately, these were shelved due to the

Action from a league game in 1928. Note the beer brand advertised on the roof frontage

outbreak of the First World War, but when peace arrived the ground underwent the first of many redevelopments which created the modern Villa Park.

Right from the start, the ground has reflected not just contemporary architectural fashions but also the club's circumstances. There have been innovations,

This view of a 1932 game provides vivid evidence of the scale of the crowds

landmarks, records set and controversy sparked. It has staged domestic and European cup finals, and internationals including European Championship and World Cup games. American football matches, boxing bouts, pop concerts and religious meetings have taken place here. In 1946, 76,588 crammed into the ground to witness an FA Cup tie against Derby

County and gates of over 40,000 were regular occurrences during the club's Third Division days. Yet the side which won the European Cup played to four-figure crowds just a few years later.

Throughout these good times and bad Villa Park has remained a landmark of English football, its proximity to the M6 making it one of the most viewed football grounds in Europe.

The Trinity Road stand, opened in 1924, boasted – in the words of author Simon Inglis – "more pomp and style" than any other. Its Italianate design, sweeping balcony, stained glass and mosaics set it apart from any other structure at any other football ground in the

VILLA PARK

BUILT: 1897 ONWARDS
LOCATION: TRINITY ROAD, BIRMINGHAM
CAPACITY: 42,788

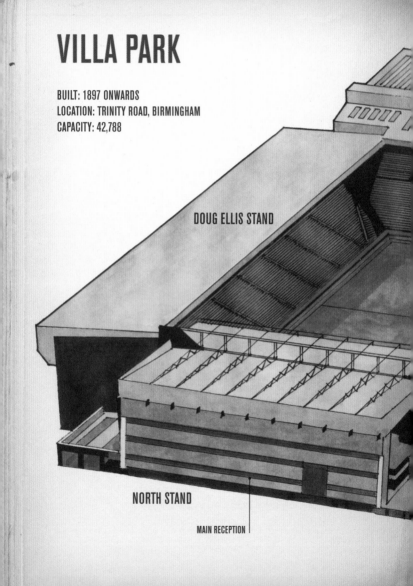

DOUG ELLIS STAND

NORTH STAND

MAIN RECEPTION

HOLTE END

TRINITY
ROAD STAND

PLAYERS' ENTRANCE

WILLIAM
MCGREGOR
STATUE

world. Its demolition in 2000 was a great shame and its successor, though impressive-looking, can never hope to leave such an impression on Villa diehards and casual fans alike.

The Witton Lane stand was the only seated area of the original Villa Park, a triple-drum roof the ground's first instantly-recognisable feature. After being repaired following bomb damage, the stand was replaced in 1963 by a small, plain and unloved structure which reflected the financial constraints of the club during this time. Then in 1993 came its successor, a double-decker affair which at the time was the largest project any football club had designed in-house.

This stand, though, went on to cause controversy, first because the city council raised objections concerning its design, then when it was given the name the Doug Ellis Stand reportedly as a 'surprise' birthday present to the then Villa chairman. Finally, complaints about legroom led to the removal of several rows of seats from the lower tier and the club being fined following the discovery of blue asbestos in the stand.

The North Stand was built on what was once the Witton End, where generations of Villa supporters ignored their first match in favour of sliding down the shale embankment at the back of the terrace. It was a revolutionary construction that reflected the

Still imposing, the modern Villa Park in 2003 hosts a game against Spurs

The new Trinity Road stand still carries plenty of presence

club's growing financial and playing confidence when it opened in 1977. It boasted the first 'goalpost' design at a British ground as well as being the first stand to have the club's initials picked out in coloured seats.

And that leaves the Holte End. First constructed as a separate entity in 1914, enlarged in 1940 (the only

example of major work at a football ground during wartime), part-covered in 1962 and fully roofed in 1990, the Holte was for many years the largest and finest end terrace in the country. The Taylor Report deemed that standing up was too dangerous at bigger grounds so, to the dismay of everyone who ever watched a match from its palatial surroundings, the Holte End was demolished in 1994. It was only fitting that its replacement should be equally grand and so it was during 1994/95 that the new Holte, at the time the largest end stand in Europe, was gradually opened.

There will be further developments at Villa Park. The North Stand, once state of the art but now looking its age, will soon be replaced. This will again give the ground a capacity of over 50,000, maybe in time to host World Cup games once more. And Villa supporters will continue to shout, cheer, sometimes complain, but above all be justifiably proud of what always has been and will remain one of the finest and most character-filled football grounds in the world.

GREAT GOALS

CHRIS NICHOLL
1977 LEAGUE CUP FINAL SECOND REPLAY V EVERTON

The final and the first replay hadn't been up to much. Villa, with several key players out through injury and by now feeling the effects of a long season, were a goal down and desperate to find a way back into the game.

Commentator John Motson described Villa's play as "still orderly and composed" as yet another attack broke down and the ball fell to centre half Chris Nicholl, out wide on the right wing. Most defenders in such a position would have hoisted another long ball high up into the penalty areas. Nicholl chose to run with the ball, beat the despairing lunge of an Everton player and fire a shot which flew off his left foot, bent in the air and screamed into the back of the net.

The distance from which the goal was scored was probably about 40 yards, an impressive feat in itself, particularly in such an important game. As is often the way, legend has exaggerated the feat, and most people who were at Old Trafford now agree that Nicholl was deep inside his own half, if not actually in the Villa penalty area, when he let fly. It was a goal fit to win a cup final and although Villa had to score two more before captain Nicholl lifted the trophy, it was his moment of triumph.

NICHOLL

NICHOLL

TONY MORLEY
1981 DIVISION ONE V EVERTON

Villa were battling for the league title with Ipswich Town when they went to Goodison Park for what promised to be a tough encounter with Everton.

The home side were always a tough test for any opponents and Villa needed to make a good start to the game in order to keep the pressure on league leaders Ipswich. 'A good start' turned out to be an understatement.

The game was just three minutes old when Gary Williams played the ball out of defence to Gary Shaw, who turned his marker and hit an inch-perfect pass to Tony Morley.

The Villa winger advanced past the halfway line and picked up the ball. He didn't actually beat any Everton defenders as none of them could get near the flying Morley, who cut inside and from 20 yards out hit a swerving drive that soared into the top corner in front of the jubilant travelling Villa support.

Villa went on to win the game 3-1 and the league title for the first time in 71 years. Morley, who had been unsure of his place in the side until the morning of the game, won the BBC Goal of the Season award for his magnificent effort. In a year of paramount team effort, it was the most outstanding moment of individual brilliance.

MORLEY.

MORLEY

SHAW

WILLIAMS

PETER WITHE
1982 EUROPEAN CUP FINAL V BAYERN MUNICH

There's not much point in saying anything about this goal. You've seen it a million times and with every single viewing you expect the ball to hit the post and bounce harmlessly out of play, don't you? Go on, admit it. But if you are the only Villa supporter living on a desert island without access to electricity and a DVD player...

The game was goalless and the team were holding on thanks to some inspired defending and Nigel Spink playing the game of his life. Then, on 67 minutes, Dennis Mortimer laid the ball off to Gary Shaw, who went wide, left Wolfgang Dremmler on the floor and passed to Tony Morley.

The Villa winger cut inside, skinned Klaus Augenthaler and slipped a pass across to the unmarked Peter Withe, seven yards out in front of goal. The ball bobbled on the uneven surface, Withe failed to make proper contact, the ball bounced off his shin, hit the inside of the post and, as time stood still, rebounded over the line.

It was never going to win any goal of the season awards. It was hardly worthy of winning a Sunday league game, never mind the European Cup. But it was, without doubt, the greatest and most important goal in the history of football. Now watch it again.

DALIAN ATKINSON
1992 PREMIER LEAGUE V WIMBLEDON

Although the season hadn't started off too well, the arrival of Dean Saunders was the catalyst that sparked one of the most fondly-remembered seasons of modern times.

He chipped in with his fair share of goals, but Saunders was just as important for his non-stop effort. It could be said that he did the work of two men, which was just as well because his partner was once of the most infuriatingly lazy footballers to ever wear claret and blue. And the main reason why he was so infuriating was because he was also one of the most talented. For most of his Villa career Dalian Atkinson was either injured or uninterested. But for a couple of months in 1992 he was something very special. And at a rain-soaked Selhurst Park he reached his peak.

Gathering the ball deep inside the Villa half Atkinson ran, and ran. Most runs of such length are the result of mazy dribbling. Atkinson charged in a straight line, beating defenders with sheer power as much as ball control.

The Wimbledon side were left in his wake, until he stopped some 25 yards from goal, then delivered a deft chip which left the goalkeeper stranded and Dalian celebrating off the pitch with a Villa supporter who was shielding him with an umbrella. Well, it was raining...

ATKINSON

SAUNDERS

ATKINSON

DWIGHT YORKE
1993 PREMIER LEAGUE V SHEFFIELD WEDNESDAY

As the race for the 1992/93 Premier League title was reaching its climax the team were playing some of the most wonderful football ever seen at Villa Park.

It seemed as though the whole side were trying to outdo each other with moments of sublime skill. At some times it was individual brilliance that lit up the game while at others, such as in the match against Sheffield Wednesday, the players combined to produce goals of stunning genius.

The game was barely two minutes old when Ray Houghton won the ball in midfield. He checked, turned and knocked the ball out to Earl Barrett, who played a short pass to Paul McGrath. The ball was then knocked around in a breathtaking mixture of first-time passing, close control, beating mesmerised opponents and finally, a centre from Steve Staunton out wide on the left wing that spilt the Wednesday defence and was hit home from short range by Dwight Yorke.

Nine players had been involved in the goal. All of them had looked in total control of the ball. The Goal of the Month award was heading once more to Villa Park, even if the Premier League trophy was destined to finish elsewhere.

After the game Ron Atkinson said, "The players are enjoying themselves." They certainly were, but surely no more than the Villa supporters.

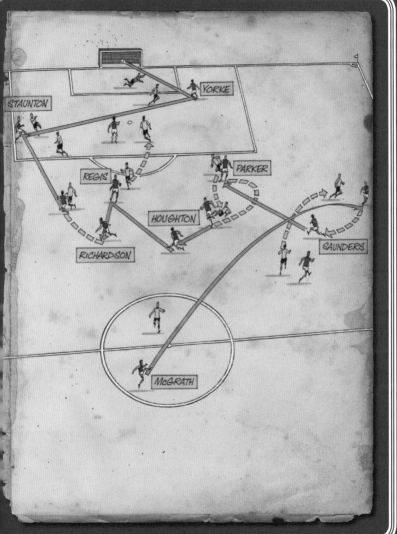

GARY CAHILL
2006 PREMIER LEAGUE V BIRMINGHAM CITY

There are few recorded instances of stunning goals in a local derby. One of the most outstanding, though, was not only a piece of individual brilliance, it was also far more important than the scorer could have realised at the time.

The score was 1-1 with 56 minutes gone and Villa were starting to come under pressure.

They pushed forward, the ball bounced around the Blues' goalmouth and out to Liam Ridgewell, who fired a hopeful cross into the box.

Kevin Phillips headed high into the air and as the ball dropped, young central defender Gary Cahill suddenly turned what was a typically scrappy move in a typically scrappy local derby into a finish more in keeping with Marco van Basten in his prime. Cahill hooked the ball from almost over his shoulder to score the first senior goal of his career.

Villa went on to win the game 3-1. Blues were relegated, with Villa not much higher in the table.

Had Cahill not scored Villa might not have won the game. Had they not taken the three points they could conceivably have been relegated.

And with Villa no longer in the Premier League would a certain rich American who was at that time looking to buy a football club in England have given them a second glance?

STILYAN PETROV
2008 PREMIER LEAGUE V DERBY COUNTY

Villa were pushing for a place in the top six while home side Derby were already relegated. In such circumstances the Rams might have been playing with the pressure off and a surprise result was a possibility. Certainly, no one at Pride Park expected Villa to run out 6-0 winners. Neither did they think they would witness one of the most memorable goals of all time, courtesy of a player who had been heavily criticised following his big money move two years earlier.

Stilyan Petrov had failed to impose himself on the Premier League after his success at Celtic, but was finally beginning to show signs of the ability that had led Martin O'Neill to make the player his first signing after becoming Villa manager.

Even so, there seemed little danger when a Derby defender passed back to goalkeeper Roy Carroll after 36 minutes with Derby already two down. Under pressure from Gabriel Agbonlahor, Carroll hit the ball upfield, straight to Petrov, who had just entered the Derby half.

The Villa player took the ball on his chest, took a step forward and fired a half-volley with his weaker left foot that flew past the stranded Carroll and into the net. Villa were three up, anther three goals were yet to come, but nothing was of any consequence except that piece of magic from Stilyan Petrov.

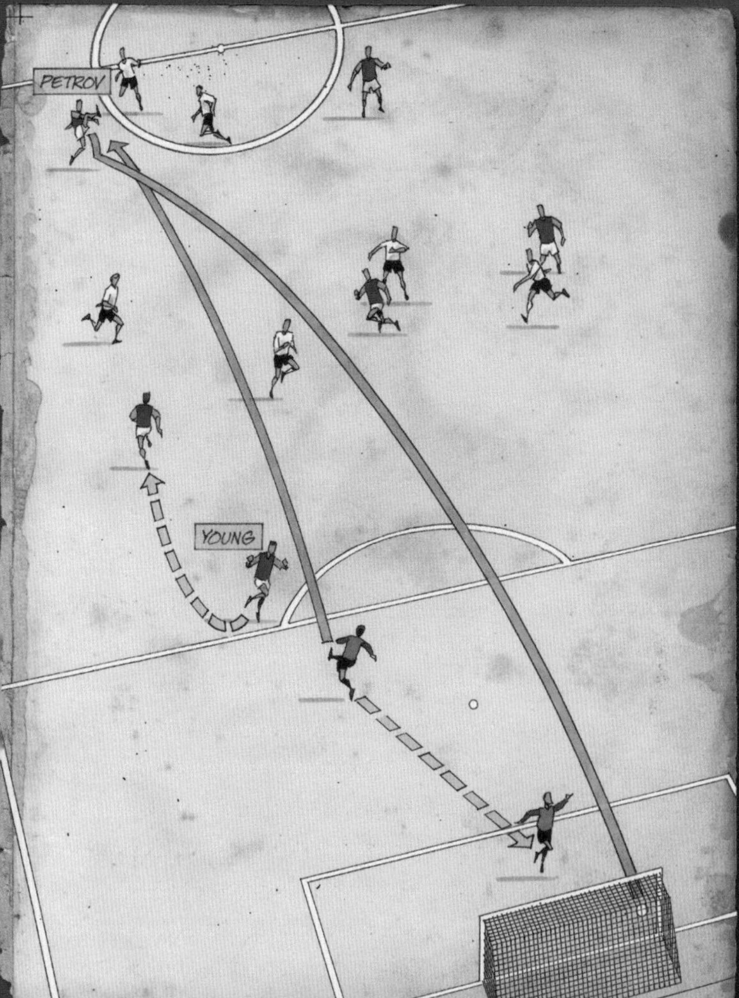
PETROV
YOUNG

RIVALRIES

The differences between football supporters in the West Midlands don't have their roots in politics or religion. There are no 'Catholic' or 'Protestant' teams, nor bitter rivalries between neighbouring towns dating back centuries. Instead supporters have tended to take as their rivals the nearest other club, or the ones they happen to be playing most often at the time.

The first competitive local derby in world football took place at Wellington Road, Perry Barr, on 19th January 1889, and saw Villa beat West Bromwich Albion 2-0. A week later the two sides played at Albion's Stoney Lane ground, drawing 3-3.

Albion were Villa's fiercest adversaries for many years, the two sides competing in three FA Cup finals with Villa winning in 1887 and 1895, Albion victorious in 1892. The reasons why Albion were Villa's first local competitors were many. For a start, they were the only club in the area to threaten Villa over a lengthy period, Small Heath being regarded as a junior club who spent much of their time in the lower divisions even after their admission to the Football League. There was also the geography of the

In the 1957 FA Cup run, Villa needed a replay to beat rivals West Brom in the semi-final

region, with Villa supporters mainly concentrated in areas such as Perry Barr and Handsworth, while Albion drew their crowds from West Bromwich and Smethwick. These areas were adjacent to each other and rivalry grew between the two clubs, particularly as during Villa's tenure at Perry Barr the district was a part of Staffordshire and separate from the city of Birmingham.

Eventually, as the club's fortunes faded in the immediate post-war era, Birmingham City, as Small Heath had become, played a much greater part in the life of Aston Villa. Again, this could have been due in part to geography. New arrivals began to make their homes in the region, so the Villa-supporting heartlands moved slightly towards areas such as Kingstanding and Erdington, which were nearer the inner-city strongholds of the club based at St Andrews. Albion, meanwhile, were finding much of their fanbase coming from deeper inside the Black Country.

The Villa-Blues competition now came to mean more to Villa than in previous years, although Albion were still fierce rivals, particularly after events in 1954 when Villa's 6-1 home win helped prevent the visitors from winning the league title. Five years later defeat at the Hawthorns condemned Villa to Division Two.

At this point Villa also had a somewhat enforced rivalry with Wolves, as the vagaries of the Football League

Captains Pat Saward (Villa) and Bill Slater (Wolves) shake before the 1960 FA Cup semi-final at The Hawthorns

Olof Mellberg scores against Wolves at Molineux in 2004

fixture compilers often pitched the two clubs against each other over the Christmas or Bank Holiday periods.

During the seventies a more tripartite challenge grew, with Villa having two clubs who saw them as increasingly bitter enemies. While they were usually able to beat the Albion (often in heated games, one of which culminated in midfielder Alex Cropley's leg being broken in a savage tackle by Albion forward Ally Brown in 1977), Villa's record against Blues was less impressive, losing five games in a row during the middle of the decade.

The early eighties saw the Villa/Blues rivalry intensifying, particularly after Ron Saunders' move across the city, and there were regular outbreaks of violence at the fixture. Albion, meanwhile, slipped off the radar of both clubs. With Villa the only local top-flight side in the area for much of the next 20 years, local derbies were restricted to cup-ties – including the never to be forgotten series in 1988 when Villa played Blues three times within a matter of weeks, winning all three games by an aggregate score of 13-0.

By the time Blues and Albion finally won promotion to the Premier League, the 'traditional' rivalry had all but disappeared as Albion had found new enemies in the shape of Black Country neighbours Wolves – that shift in population coming into play once more. Villa's relationship with Blues, on the other hand, had intensified into something very nasty, manifesting itself in the two league clashes of 2002/03 which took place against a backdrop of violence around the grounds, pitch invasions and two Villa players being sent off. Blues had the better of the first few games during this resumption but recent seasons have seen the balance shift, with Villa's 1-0 win in April 2010 marking their sixth successive victory over the team who are now their deadliest and only real rivals.

Despite the longstanding and sometimes hostile element to the rivalry there has never been any bar to the clubs buying players from each other. In the early days many successful Villa players, such as Denny Hodgetts and Charlie Athersmith, ended their careers at Small Heath while Villa's Peter Withe had played for Blues in his earlier days. Ron Saunders' tour of the managerial hot seats led to several of his former players signing for Blues or Albion, and in the case of Robert Hopkins, both. In recent years, Villa have sold several players to Blues, including Kevin Phillips, Liam Ridgewell and, most recently, Craig Gardner, for considerable sums. Football may be one thing, but business is still business.

Derbies against Birmingham have become highly-charged affairs

ASTON VILLA COMIC STRIP HISTORY 2

AFTER WINNING THE FA CUP IN 1895 VILLA ALLOWED THE TROPHY TO BE DISPLAYED IN THE SHOP WINDOW OF A LOCAL SPORTS OUTFITTER, WHO SUPPLIED THE TEAM WITH THEIR BOOTS,

UNFORTUNATELY ONE NIGHT THE CUP WAS STOLEN, AND DESPITE A HUGE (FOR THE TIME) REWARD IT WAS NEVER FOUND...

VILLA WERE FINED BY THE FA AND ORDERED TO PAY FOR A NEW TROPHY.

NOTHING MORE WAS HEARD AND THE CRIME REMAINED A MYSTERY FOR OVER SIXTY YEARS,

THEN ONE DAY IN 1958 AN OLD LAG 'CONFESSED' TO HAVING STOLEN THE CUP, AND SAID HE HAD BROKEN IT DOWN TO MAKE COUNTERFEIT COINS...

WHICH HE AND HIS ACCOMPLICES THEN PASSED OFF IN THE PUB OWNED BY VILLA FORWARD DENNY HODGETTS.

THE STORY OF THE VILLA
FROM WAR TO REVOLUTION
1914-68

Life at Villa Park seemed to have regained its normal, triumphal, pace as football resumed after the First World War. Villa won the FA Cup for the sixth time by beating Huddersfield Town in 1920, after which the President of the Football League, Mr J Kenna, called them the 'gramophone club' – they were "always setting records."

In 1924 Villa made their first appearance at the new Wembley. Although they lost that FA Cup final to Newcastle United, few doubted it would be long before the team returned to the Empire Stadium in triumph. Little did they know.

By now Frederick Rinder was the driving force behind Villa's administration and although ambitious plans to expand Villa Park to hold 130,000 had been cancelled due to the war, Rinder forced through the building of the new Trinity Road stand. This magnificent construction with its Italianate staircase and stained glass windows was without doubt the most magnificent stand in the world at the time, but it was also vastly over budget and was the cause of Rinder being forced to resign from the board in 1925.

Villa's league form was consistent

if not earth-shattering during this time, but the early
1930s saw a period during which they came close
to emulating the successes of the Victorian era. In
1930/31 the team scored 128 league goals but could
only finish runners-up to Arsenal – 49 of those goals
came from Thomas 'Pongo' Waring. Other star names
of the period included Eric Houghton, who went on
to serve the club for over 50 years, and Billy Walker,
said by many to be the finest Villa player of them all.
The team also finished runners-up in 1932/33, again
to Arsenal, but decline was swift and in 1936 the Villa

Prince Henry meets the
Villa players before the
1920 FA Cup final at
Stamford Bridge

From left: Broome, Haycock, Shell, Starling and Houghton at The Valley in 1938

found themselves relegated to Division Two after a horrendous season in which they conceded no less than 110 goals in 42 league games.

It's difficult to exaggerate the impact that Villa's relegation had on the greater footballing public. Imagine Liverpool going straight through the current divisions into the Conference and you might get somewhere near it. Yet, not for the last time, Villa reacted by seizing the opportunity for innovation and hired the noted coach Jimmy Hogan as manager. Hogan was well-known on the Continent although his revolutionary ways were hard for the traditionalists in English football. So, in a way that would be repeated over half a century later, a Villa manager found himself ahead of his time. Hogan was able to put together a team capable of winning the Second Division title in 1938 and establish themselves back in the top flight before fate, in the shape of Adolf Hitler and his plans for another sort of domination, took a hand.

At the start of the First World War, Villa had a promising team. Once football restarted in peacetime the side was older and replacements difficult to find. Big money was occasionally spent on players, usually when relegation threatened once more, but there was a lethargy around the club. Danny Blanchflower, one of the greatest footballers of his era, arrived from Barnsley but soon left, bemoaning the way the club was run. Peter McParland, the only player of the time to rival Blanchflower in terms of ability, stayed but later voiced similar criticisms. In short, the board were stuck in the days when Aston Villa was the foremost name in world football. Their ways, they reasoned, were tried and trusted ones and the poor run the club was enduring was merely a temporary problem.

In hindsight, 1957's record seventh FA Cup win, and in particular the 2-1 victory over Manchester United in the final, merely papered over the cracks. Manager Eric Houghton resigned less than two years later, to be replaced by Joe Mercer. Villa were unluckily relegated at the end of 1958/59 under Mercer, made an immediate return as Second Division champions and won the inaugural League Cup in 1960/61. Houghton had revived Villa's policy of encouraging youth and this was to pay dividends over the next few years as the 'Mercer Minors,' as the team were dubbed, contained a host of promising young players. But several of them were to suffer serious injuries and the team's promise, rich though it was, faded. Mercer was sacked during the summer of 1964, after recovering from what was later revealed to be a minor stroke. His subsequent success at Manchester City showed how short-sighted the Villa directors had been in getting rid of him.

If the board had been old-fashioned during the 1950s, they were positively antiquated during the following decade as football evolved at an ever-increasing pace. The well-meaning but utterly out-of-touch collection of local worthies proved totally incapable of running what could still described without fear of contradiction as the best-known name in English football.

Further relegation came in 1967. Unlike on the two previous occasions, no one was under any illusion that there would be a quick return. That the best they could obtain in the way of a new manager was Tommy Cummings from Mansfield Town showed how low the Villa's fortunes had fallen and, while Cummings

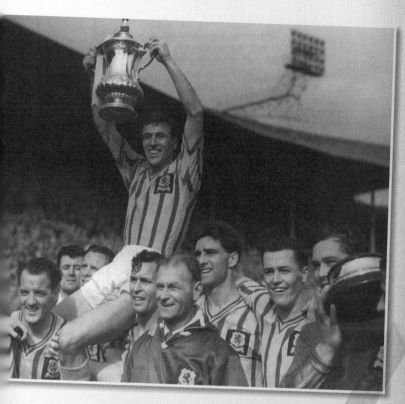

himself was well-meaning and made several shrewd
signings, by November 1968 Villa were that most
modern of journalistic clichés, a club in crisis.
Supporters were protesting both inside the ground and
at a meeting held at Digbeth Civic Hall, Cummings

Johnny Dixon holds the
FA Cup after Villa won
the 1957 final to secure
a record seventh win

was dismissed and eventually,
the board agreed to step
aside in order to let a new
regime be given the task of reviving
the fortunes of the club.

 After weeks of speculation, it was revealed
that a consortium headed by local businessman
and former Birmingham City director Douglas Ellis
were to be the club's new owners. Their first act was to
appoint the controversial Tommy Docherty as manager.
Within days the very soul of Aston Villa FC would be
shaken to its Victorian foundations.

Floodlit derby action
against West Brom
in 1965

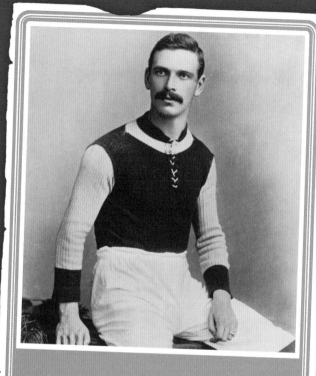

KIT PARADE

Aston Villa. Claret and blue. The two go together. But it hasn't always been the case – in their early days the team wore many different colours and designs, while several of the more recent shirts have featured designs that are anything but the traditional claret body and blue arms that have been made so famous by generations of Villa players.

Red and blue hoops, all-claret, all-black and blue and white hoops were some of Villa's colours in those pioneering mid-Victorian years, and although the team first came to fame wearing claret and blue in winning the 1887 FA Cup final, the design was a strange striped affair which would only last for a season.

Then came chocolate and blue halves, claret and blue, claret and blue halves and a return to chocolate and blue once more before, in 1893, the team celebrated their first league title with the familiar colours which they were to wear from then on.

Many theories have been put forward as to why claret and blue were adopted as the Villa's colours. It is believed that commercial artist Ollie

The Villa's kit as worn in 1891/92

Wheatley, a Villa player in the 1880s, was responsible for designing the first claret and blue kit the club wore, although why he chose these colours is not known – maybe his professional eye just saw how good they looked together.

The design of claret body and light blue arms was then worn, with few alterations, until 1956. So famous did this classic design become, and so envied were the Villa club, that many others emulated them.

West Ham United began wearing claret and blue after one of their players won a bet with a Villa counterpart, the wager being a set of shirts. And it was reputed that Arsenal began wearing white sleeves as their manager Herbert Chapman was a great admirer of the Villa and wished to make his own team's shirts more like the Midlands club's.

Minor changes to the kit occurred during this time – mainly to the design of the collar – while from 1900 to 1923 Villa wore claret socks with blue trim as opposed to the black with claret and blue trim favoured in other years.

The first major change to the Villa kit in the 20th century was unveiled in 1956. The shirt was changed from a round to a v-necked collar, it was no longer buttoned and the club badge was featured regularly

The 1957 FA Cup final shirt

for the first time. Claret and blue socks were introduced in the following year and this kit was to remain more or less unchanged until 1969, although a subtle change saw white socks brought in from 1965-68.

The new broom that was sweeping clean at Villa Park during this period also provided a new kit design. Shirts were all-claret with blue trim, while the collar was now blocked rather than cut. The most sweeping change occurred with the introduction of a new away kit, which in contrast to the white Villa had traditionally used until this point was the same design as the first choice, but in yellow and royal blue. So radical was this change that Villa were booed onto the pitch before a pre-season friendly against the Italian under-21 side at Villa Park, the crowds mistaking their own team for the visitors.

White socks and shirts were introduced to the home kit in 1970 and it remained unaltered until 1975. The new shirt was not significantly different. The collar became a claret and blue striped affair, while the club badge changed to the round shield and for the first time the trademark of a manufacturer, in this case the diamond of Umbro, was featured. But this was, without doubt, the classic Villa kit of the modern era. Complete with its away variation of white with claret and blue along the arms (another nod to growing commercialisation), this was the shirt in which Villa gained promotion, won two League Cups and became league champions once more. It was a shirt to wear and imagine you were Gary Shaw, the hottest property in English football.

The league champions defended their title in a new design, claret with blue arms and side panels, featuring the logo of manufacturers Le Coq Sportif on both arms. Additions for the following season were the name of Davenport's, the club's first shirt sponsors, and the words 'Champions of Europe'.

In 1983/84 came the most revolutionary change to the Villa kit in 90 years, with a shadow-striped design of a predominantly claret body, the only blue being on side panels. This also featured the logo of Mita, who remained Villa's sponsors for years.

This was followed in 1985/86 by a shirt which

Gary Shaw grins and bears the infamous 1987 'blancmange' shirt design

Lee Hendrie in the popular 2002 retro kit

was claret with blue trim and featured the name of Mita and manufacturers Henson, along with AVFC – but no club badge.

Controversial though this move was, it was as nothing compared to the half-striped 'blancmange' Hummel design foisted on the club from 1987-89 and which new manager Graham Taylor made clear would be changed as soon as possible. It was, and 1989/90 saw a more traditional claret body, blue arms and white shorts with blue socks, albeit with manufacturer's and sponsor's names featuring prominently. After a brief change from 1990-92, the 1992/93 season saw a retro-design with a lace collar and new badge. This lasted just a season, and in its place came an unpopular claret and blue striped affair.

We were well into the era of football kits as leisurewear by now and as sales expanded, so did the number of shirts available. Three kits a year became the norm, with Villa having had more different designs since the Premier League was formed than any other club. Some have been traditional (the 2002/03 Fifties-style offering was well-received) while the least said about others the better. There was a time when Villa seemed determined to give the shirt a striped design whenever possible. At other times the leisurewear mentality held sway, giving the away kit in particular a host of designs and colours that Villa men of days gone by would have had difficulty recognising as connected to the sport in general, let alone their club.

The past few years have seen Villa revert to the traditional claret body/blue sleeves look. Modern fashions and the need to maximise revenue means there will always be additional features, and advertising on the shirt is here to stay – although Villa made a wonderful gesture in donating their shirt sponsorship to children's charity Acorns from 2008 – but at least a Villa shirt is still immediately recognisable.

The 2004 variation of the classic Villa colours

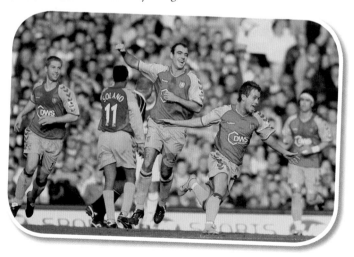

HALL OF FAME

CHARLIE AITKEN

Charlie made his league debut in 1961 in a game against Sheffield Wednesday that saw the final first-team appearance of Johnny Dixon.

Charlie evidently impressed, becoming Villa's first-choice left back from then until midway through the 1975/76 season. So he witnessed a period of turbulence as great as any club has ever undergone – the brief flowering of the Mercer Minors and their decline, the club's fall through to the Third Division and the subsequent recovery.

Off the field, widespread supporter dissatisfaction led to protests against the board and the eventual arrival of Doug Ellis's new broom.

Through it all, Charlie Aitken remained a model of consistency on the left hand side of Villa's defence.

Charlie stayed with the Villa throughout the dark days of the Second and Third divisions, never once thinking that his career might be better served elsewhere, and turning down moves to better clubs on more than one occasion.

He began his career at a time when full backs still had just two roles during a match – tackle the winger and then get rid of the ball. Like many of his contemporaries, Charlie undoubtedly struggled for a while when the changing nature of the game meant he was expected to do his share of attacking, but he adapted to the role.

Towards the end of his career he was still making runs along the wing with a regularity that would tax players ten years his junior.

This remarkable level of fitness was Charlie's greatest asset. For many years he was the quickest man on Villa's books and even if an opponent got past him they would often find themselves being caught up again and tackled.

Equally, he was able to shrug off injuries that would have sidelined many a lesser player. This was one of the reasons why he was able to boast such an impressive record of appearances, breaking the record held by Billy Walker in 1974.

Charlie was granted a free transfer two years later, a move to New York Cosmos ending the career of one of the Villa's greatest servants.

Born: Edinburgh, 1st May 1942

Aston Villa appearances: 656

Aston Villa goals: 16

Honours won with Aston Villa: League Cup (1975)

Other clubs: New York Cosmos (1976)

International appearances: None

CHARLIE AITKEN FACTFILE

CHARLIE ATHERSMITH

At the end of the 19th century the Villa outside right was widely regarded as the finest footballer in the world.

Newspapers and weekly sporting journals filled their pages with stories of the most popular football club in the country and Athersmith was rarely given a critical press. There are few mentions of him losing the ball, hardly any of him delivering a less than accurate cross to his forwards.

He made his first-team debut aged just 18, and for the next 11 years hardly missed a game as Villa cemented their place as the pre-eminent force in English football. The club won five league titles and the FA Cup on two occasions during this period and Athersmith formed a devastating partnership with club captain and inside right John Devey. Charlie's prowess did not go unnoticed by the England selectors and he made his international debut against Ireland in 1892. Indeed, during Villa's double-winning season of

1896/97, Athersmith performed a unique feat. In addition to gaining league and FA Cup winners' medals, he played for England in all three internationals and represented the Football League against the Scottish League. No other player has won every honour available in a season.

Athersmith undoubtedly relied on his blistering speed to best most defenders. That said, he was also blessed with devastating ball control and no mean ability to deliver an inch-perfect cross. Rarely did a full back manage to stop Charlie, and if one did it was invariably by foul means.

But all good things must come to an end and Charlie moved to Small Heath in 1901. Although they continued to regularly win trophies for over a decade, Villa were not the same force without him.

As for the most notable story surrounding Charlie's career, that during a rainstorm he was handed an umbrella by a member of the crowd and continued playing while at the same time sheltering from the elements, no one has ever been able to find any proof of the tale. It must go down as yet another legend to add to the many surrounding Villa in the Victoria era.

> **One of the fleetest right-wingers of his time. With a working partner he was well-nigh irresistible**
> *The Aston Villa News & Record,*
> September 1906

Born: Bloxwich, Staffs, 10th May 1872

Aston Villa appearances: 307

Aston Villa goals: 85

Honours won with Aston Villa: **League Championship** (1894, 1896, 1897, 1899, 1900), FA Cup (1895, 1897)

Other clubs: **Small Heath Alliance** (1901-05)

International appearances: England, 12, 3 goals

CHARLIE ATHERSMITH FACTFILE

GORDON COWANS

In 1975 a wide-eyed 16-year-old arrived at Villa Park to begin what was then still called an apprenticeship.

He's still there now and if we ignore those brief occasions when he left, only to return when the lure of the claret and blue proved too strong, Gordon Cowans is part of a three-man chain that goes back 60 years. The careers of Johnny Dixon, Charlie Aitken and Gordon overlap to form a link stretching back to the final days of the Second World War, and there can be few clubs in the world with such a claim.

Cowans, known from that first day as Sid, burst onto the scene during Villa's League Cup-winning year of 1977. He made 215 consecutive appearances in four seasons from 1979-83, winning the Robinsons' Barley Water Young Player of the Year in 1979/80. Not only a fearsome tackler for his size, Cowans could pass the ball as well as anyone.

Gordon Cowans became the complete central

midfielder. He was at the peak of his ability in 1982/83, the finest playmaker in the league, gaining an international call-up and the subject of a bid from Napoli which would have taken his wage earnings into levels unheard of at that time in England. Unfortunately, a vicious tackle shattered his leg during a pre-season tournament in Barcelona.

Cowans made a full recovery but was then sold to Seri A club Bari. Then in 1988, with Villa promoted from Division Two, manager Graham Taylor was looking to add experience to his youthful side and Cowans fitted the bill. Alongside the emerging talents of David Platt, he flourished again.

Villa struggled against relegation for much of 1990/91, but Cowans remained on top form. The arrival of Ron Atkinson led to him joining Blackburn Rovers for £200,000 but two years later Cowans returned to Villa again for a short period.

After hanging up his boots Cowans was a coach with Burnley for a while, but it was no surprise when he returned to Villa Park for a fourth time to become coach of the club's Youth Academy.

> **❝ My greatest ambition? To make a run Gordon Cowans doesn't spot ❞**
> David Platt

Born: West Cornfirth, Co Durham, 27th October 1958

Aston Villa appearances: 506

Aston Villa goals: 59

Honours won with Aston Villa: European Super Cup (1983), European Cup (1982), Football League (1981), League Cup (1977)

Other clubs: Bari (1985), Blackburn Rovers (1991), Derby County (1994), Wolverhampton Wanderers (1994), Sheffield United (1995), Bradford City (1996), Stockport County (1997), Burnley (1997)

International appearances: England, 10, 2 goals

GORDON COWANS FACTFILE

PAUL MCGRATH

Words like 'legend' and 'world-class' have lost their meaning in the hype-driven world of modern football.

It's therefore difficult to put Paul McGrath into perspective to anyone who didn't see him play. If you were one of those unfortunates then no, it's not an exaggeration. Yes, he was that good.

And of course those stories are true.

Graham Taylor paid £425,000 to bring McGrath to Villa Park in the summer of 1989, smashing the club's wage structure to land the player.

Paul turned up drunk to sign for the club, attempted suicide in his first few weeks and played while under the influence. The omens were not good, yet Taylor managed to rescue McGrath from the abyss; Villa physio Jim Walker did the same with his fragile body.

These two men got McGrath performing to the best of his massive ability, Villa finished the season runners-up to

Liverpool and Paul was voted Villa Player of the Year. He went on to win the award six years in succession.

Throughout the rollercoaster ride of the Venglos and Atkinson years McGrath didn't train, there were reports of his being carried unconscious out of pubs throughout Birmingham and on more than one occasion he missed games, whereabouts unknown. None of this mattered a great deal because during that time Paul McGrath was the finest central defender in England, if not the world. His timing was majestic, his ability to intimidate opposing forwards unparalleled. It was said, only half in jest, that McGrath's tackling was the only question mark about his game, because he never had to make a tackle.

As the years went by and Paul's physical powers lessened, he changed his game to suit his physical ability. One particular trick he perfected was the ability to back-heel the ball if he was ever wrong-sided; he could perform this trick better than most players could kick normally.

The start of the 1996/97 season saw McGrath unable to get into the side and he moved to Derby County for £100,000.

> **ff Paul McGrath is one of the all-time greats. Someone to compare with Bobby Moore JJ**
> Jack Charlton

PAUL MCGRATH FACTFILE

Born: Ealing, 4th December 1959

Aston Villa appearances: 315
Aston Villa goals: 9

Honours won with Aston Villa: League Cup (1994, 1996)

Other clubs: St Patrick's Athletic (1981), Manchester United (1982), Derby County (1996), Sheffield United (1997)

International appearances: Republic of Ireland, 83, 8 goals

PETER McPARLAND

Much of Peter's fame is, of course, down to the 1957 FA Cup final, when he injured Manchester United goalkeeper Ray Wood with a challenge that was perfectly legal if not entirely ethical, and then compounded the insult by scoring the two goals that brought the cup back to what was then its favourite home.

But that wonderful afternoon was just one part of the Peter McParland story.

In a way, Peter's most notable achievement was also his biggest handicap, as the memory of it often overshadows his other achievements.

Villa have never had a better winger, and few can claim to have been his equal. He played at centre forward for Northern Ireland in the 1958 World Cup finals, eminent Villa historian Peter Morris reckoning him the club's finest in that position since Pongo Waring. No less an authority than Danny Blanchflower regarded Peter as the best inside forward in the world.

Between the 'nearly side' of the 1930s and the European

Champions of 50 years later there was no Villa player held in greater esteem.

> **" Stop McParland and you stop the Villa "**
> Almost every opposition manager

Persuading McParland to sign for the Villa was not difficult as he grew up in Northern Ireland with a father away in Birmingham on war work. Sent a copy of the *Sports Argus* every week, the youngster inevitably became a Villa supporter.

McParland joined Villa in August 1952, making his debut almost immediately, but took a while to get settled into the side. Once established, Peter became a favourite with the Villa Park crowds.

He was never a particularly skilful ball player, relying on drive and determination to beat defenders. Peter regularly found himself finishing a move as well as starting it, cutting in and firing off a fearsome shot as often as he would make for the by-line to cross.

Now living in retirement on the south coast, he still visits Villa Park regularly, and the site of such a footballing God walking across the North Stand car park invariably brings out a cluster of autograph hunters spanning the generations.

He also has one more footballing ambition – "To see another Villa player score the winner in the cup final."

Born: **Newry, Co Down** 25th April 1934

Aston Villa appearances: 340

Aston Villa goals: 120

Honours won with Aston Villa: **FA Cup** (1957), League Cup (1961)

Other clubs: Dundalk (1950), Wolverhampton Wanderers (1962), Plymouth Argyle (1963), Atlanta Chiefs (1967)

International appearances: Northern Ireland, 34, 10 goals

PETER McPARLAND FACTFILE

DENNIS MORTIMER

On 23rd December 1975, Ron Saunders spent what was then a club record fee of £175,000 on what he described as a "Christmas present for the fans."

Saunders would have known he was buying a top-class midfielder, but he could never have guessed he was signing a player who was to become the most successful Villa captain of the past 100 years.

Mortimer immediately became a mainstay of the side. His surging runs from midfield were just one part of his game; he also had a shot that could rival the best and was no mean tackler. For seven years, if he wasn't the best central midfielder in the country he was certainly the most consistent.

In 1980/81 the side won their place in history as league champions and although Gary Shaw and Peter Withe grabbed the headlines week after week it was their captain who provided the most telling image of all with his decisive goal at home to Liverpool.

Villa's midfield was the perfect balance; the artistry of Gordon Cowans and the industry of Des Bremner blended perfectly with Mortimer's drive. If anything, though, Dennis's finest quality was his leadership. Never was the phrase 'midfield general' a more apt description. He would argue that the team he captained had 11 captains, but Dennis Mortimer was truly first amongst equals.

Mortimer's leadership qualities were utilised in another way in 1981/82. The shock departure of Ron Saunders left his assistant Tony Barton in charge, and although Barton deserves immense credit for the way he steered the club towards the greatest night in its history, his task would not have been possible without the work done by Dennis Mortimer in ensuring the players remained focussed on winning the biggest prize in club football.

However, as a close ally of Ron Saunders he was never going to get on with the returning Doug Ellis. The sacking of Tony Barton in 1984 meant Mortimer's days at Villa Park were numbered. New manager Graham Turner wasted no time in easing him out of the club at the first opportunity. It was an ignominious end to one of the great Villa careers.

> **ff Dennis WAS Aston Villa**
> Tony Morley **JJ**

Born: Liverpool, 5th April 1952

Aston Villa appearances: 405

Aston Villa goals: 36

Honours won with Aston Villa: European Super Cup (1983), European Cup (1982), Football League (1981)

Other clubs: Coventry City (1969), Sheffield United (1985 - loan), Brighton (1985), Birmingham City (1986)

International appearances: None

DENNIS MORTIMER FACTFILE

DAVID PLATT

David Platt's arrival at Villa Park was unheralded. His departure made headlines around Europe.

In between he became one of the most significant footballers in the history of the modern English game.

Platt signed from Crewe in February 1988 for £200,000. He was described by manager Graham Taylor at the time as "overpriced" but proved to be one of the biggest bargains the Villa have ever struck. Platt's impact was immediate; he scored on his debut away at Blackburn Rovers, got the only goal in Villa's decisive win at home to Bradford City and netted five in 11 games as Villa returned to the First Division.

The following season saw Platt emerge as a top class midfielder, scoring 15 goals as Villa narrowly escaped relegation and in 1989/90 he became a star.

For Villa he was immense, his late runs into the penalty area to get onto the end of Gordon Cowans' sublime passes a feature of the team's title challenge.

Called into the England squad for Italia 90 his last minute winner against Belgium would in ordinary circumstances have been a remarkable goal. In the context of what came next, it was the most important scored by the national side since 1966. The team eventually returned home as gallant heroes and David Platt's international career was assured.

In 1990/91 Villa struggled to maintain the standards of the previous season. Platt was on even better form, but the team spirit which had been a feature of the side under Graham Taylor was beginning to wear thin. It became clear towards the end of the season that Platt was off to Italy. He eventually signed for Bari, the fee of £5.5 million by far the biggest involving a British player at that time.

He had helped Villa get out of the Second Division and almost win the league title. The money received from his transfer helped finance Ron Atkinson's successful team. And he was Villa's first real star for many years.

But it was that one goal in Italy which ensured Platt's place in history. English football would today be very different were it not for David Platt.

> **❝ The last player I have to worry about is David Platt ❞**
> Graham Taylor

Born: Chadderton, Lancs, 10th August 1966

Aston Villa appearances: 145

Aston Villa goals: 68

Honours won with Aston Villa: European Super Cup (1983), European Cup (1982), Football League (1981)

Other clubs: Manchester United (1982), Crewe Alexandra (1985), Bari (1991), Juventus (1992), Sampdoria (1993), (Arsenal 1995), Nottingham Forest (1999)

International appearances: England, 62, 27 goals

DAVID PLATT FACTFILE

BILLY WALKER

W. WALKER.

Villa legend Eric Houghton called Billy "The finest footballer I have ever seen."

Over half a century later *Times* writer Richard Whitehead had Billy at number one on his list of 50 Greatest Villa Players.

When these and countless other tributes are considered it's fair to call Billy Walker the strongest candidate for the title of Aston Villa's best-ever player.

He made his debut in 1920 against Queens Park Rangers in the FA Cup, scoring two goals, and continued to find the net regularly throughout his first season, which ended with an FA Cup winner's medal after victory in the final over Newcastle. At this time Billy was a centre forward but the departure of Clem Stephenson led to his moving to inside left. It was here that his reputation was made, although his time in the centre gave him an ability in the air which he never lost.

No other playing honours were to come Billy's way after Villa's defeat by Huddersfield Town in the 1924 FA Cup final. The team settled into what would now be regarded as a consistent top six position, although only in the brief period from 1930-33 did they ever look like adding to the club's trophy haul.

Billy was always good for a double figure tally of goals per season, often netting 20 or more, and laid on many of the goals for his free-scoring team-mates. A magnificent ball player, Walker was worshipped by the Villa Park crowds in a way that no player had been since Harry Hampton.

He scored on his international debut, against Ireland in 1920, and his last cap came against Austria in 1932, at the age of 35. He was the first England player to score at Wembley, against Scotland in 1924, and once went in goal during an international, when England played France in 1925. His number of first team appearances has only been surpassed by Charlie Aitken, and his tally of 244 goals may never be beaten.

The best Villa player of all time? It's difficult to find a better candidate.

> **He can as near as does not matter make a football do parlour tricks, sit up and beg and follow him if he whistled**
>
> Roland Allen, *The Times*

BILLY WALKER FACTFILE

Born: Wednesbury, Staffs, 29th October 1897
Aston Villa appearances: 531
Aston Villa goals: 244
Honours won with Aston Villa: FA Cup (1920)
Other clubs: None
International appearances: England, 18, 9 goals

THOMAS 'PONGO' WARING

T. WARING
ASTON VILLA F.C

Thomas Waring, known to everyone in the football world as 'Pongo,' arrived at Villa Park in February 1928, costing £4,700 from Tranmere Rovers.

Five days after signing he turned out in a Central League fixture against Birmingham City which drew a crowd of 23,000 to Villa Park. He scored a first-half hat-trick. He was in the first team the following Saturday and rarely out of it for years.

Stranding over six feet tall, Pongo's ability to handle the most physical of centre halves was well-known but he was also a very shrewd footballer. If the opposition were able to cut off the line of supply to the Villa attack he would willingly drop back and collect the ball, unlike most centre forwards of the era, who rarely ventured into their own half.

Waring's goalscoring record was phenomenal throughout his Villa career. He reached his peak in

1930/31 with 49 in the league and a further goal in the FA Cup and should have been an England regular, but his temperamental nature was of concern to the FA selection committee.

Billy Walker, his team captain for many years, said of Waring: "There were no rules for Pongo. Nobody knew what time he would turn up for training, nobody could do anything with him." But Pongo balanced these outbursts with a sense of fun. He was a hugely likeable character, popular with his team-mates due to his larger than life personality.

From 1932 onwards Pongo's appearances were less frequent even though his scoring record was as reliable as ever. For some inexplicable reason Villa manager Jimmy McMullen sold him after a good start to 1935/36 and he moved to Barnsley in November 1935. Villa were relegated at the end of the season.

As a postscript, during the Second World War Pongo was playing for New Brighton when he recommended a couple of players to the Villa, agreeing to play alongside them in a reserve game at Villa Park. The match attracted a crowd over 20,000 and kick-off had to be delayed until Waring had finished signing autographs.

> **❝ He got the name because of his malodorous feet ❞**
> Gilbert Odd, Tranmere Rovers historian

PONGO WARING FACTFILE

Born: Birkenhead, 12th October 1906

Aston Villa appearances: 226

Aston Villa goals: 167

Honours won with Aston Villa: None

Other clubs: Tranmere Rovers (1926), Barnsley (1935), Wolverhampton Wanderers (1936), Tranmere Rovers (1936), Accrington Stanley (1938)

International appearances: England, 5, 4 goals

DWIGHT YORKE

We can look at Dwight in two ways. There was the star of Villa's briefly flourishing mid-nineties side, or there was the player damned by supporters for

the way he moved to Manchester United and for his subsequent actions.

What is definite is that following his arrival in 1989, Yorke began to make progress, not least during 1991/92 when he became a first team regular and won the Villa Young Player of the Year award.

He was also starting to play an important part in Villa's title challenge the following season when for some reason he was dropped and found it difficult to get back into the side.

Although his commitment was never faulted Dwight gave little indication that he would be anything more than another promising youngster who failed to make the final breakthrough.

Brian Little became Villa manager and one genius promptly recognised another. Played as an out and out striker from the start of 1995/96 Yorke scored 25 goals.

There were headers, long-range shots, tap-ins, a goal in the 3-0 demolition of Leeds in the League Cup final and a chipped penalty against Sheffield United that barely crossed the goalline.

> **If he makes a first division footballer my name's Mao Tse Tung**
>
> Tommy Docherty

For two seasons Villa were considered likely challengers to Manchester United and the fact that Yorke couldn't stop scoring was a major contributory factor.

Then came the arrival of Stan Collymore and the ensuing fallout. Dwight was dropped back into midfield and although his workrate was once more beyond question, it took Little's resignation and the appointment of John Gregory to get Yorke back on form.

Sadly for the Villa though, his head was gradually being turned in the direction of Manchester.

The whole affair was drawn-out, messy and badly-organised on all sides until the inevitable move to Old Trafford, for £12.6 million. The passage of time has helped calm some of the vitriol felt toward Dwight Yorke by Villa fans and now we can maybe see him for what he was – one of the finest strikers the club has ever produced and one of the few modern-day Villa players who could truly be called world class.

Born: Canaan, Tobago, 3rd November 1971

Aston Villa appearances: 247

Aston Villa goals: 97

Honours won with Aston Villa: League Cup (1996)

Other clubs: Manchester United (1998), Blackburn Rovers (2002), Birmingham City (2004), Sydney (2005), Sunderland (2006)

International appearances: Trinidad & Tobago, 72, 19 goals

DWIGHT YORKE FACTFILE

THE THIRD DEGREE

CHESTERFIELD
FOOTBALL
CLUB LTD.

Season 1970-71

Official Programme One Shilling

v

ASTON VILLA

SATURDAY, 15th AUGUST, 1970   Kick-off 3.15

FOOTBALL LEAGUE   THIRD DIVISION

Registered Office: SALTERGATE, CHESTERFIELD. Telephone 2219

It was the best of times, it was the worst of times…

Big clubs playing below what they regard as their natural level has always been a feature of English football. Manchester City and Nottingham Forest were in what used to be called Division Three not so long ago while even the self-styled Greatest Club in the World™ suffered the ignominy of relegation as recently as 1974.

But there has never been a bigger fish in a small footballing pool as there was during the two bittersweet seasons Aston Villa spent in the Third Division. The world woke up to this new phenomenon on the opening day of 1970/71, when Villa were due to play away at Chesterfield. With New Street station mobbed, British Rail raised their prices in an attempt to limit the numbers travelling. It was to no avail; police and club officials used to dealing with a couple of hundred visiting fans found themselves powerless as Villa supporters took over Chesterfield's Saltergate ground. As fighting broke out manager Vic Crowe was forced to appeal for calm. That afternoon 16,760 turned up, Chesterfield's next home game attracted a crowd less than half the size.

This was to be just the start of two incredible seasons in which Villa smashed all sorts of records for attendance, spending and points gained, as well as providing supporters with some of their fondest memories.

The 1970/71 season was predominantly about the League Cup. Villa advanced to the semi-finals and a date with Manchester United. At Old Trafford, 49,000 saw a 1-1 draw. The second leg, a few days before Christmas, provided a gate of 62,500 for a memorable match in which Villa went a goal down before running out 2-1 winners over a United side featuring Best, Law and Charlton. The scenes of jubilation were such as few grounds have ever witnessed.

The final saw Villa outplay Spurs for much of the match only to go down to two late goals from Martin Chivers as the Villa fans completely drowned out the winners from the moment Wembley's gates opened until the last supporter had left.

The cup run had an effect on league performances and this led to the team finishing a disappointing fourth in the final table. Any feeling of unease was soon swept away as Villa began the following campaign in fine style. Attendances at Villa Park, already high, were soon to break all records. The top of the table clash with Bournemouth attracted 48,110, while shortly afterwards 54,437 paid club record gate receipts to watch a friendly against Santos. In nine days Villa had attracted over 100,000 to the ground – several clubs in the division struggled to attract that number over the course of the season. Such income did, of course, give Villa a massive advantage over their rivals and they made the most of their financial muscle. Jim Cumbes and Ian Ross arrived from First Division clubs West Brom and Liverpool respectively. Ross's £70,000 fee was the highest ever paid by a Third Division club, this record lasting all of a week before it was exceeded by the £90,000 paid to Luton Town for Chris Nicholl. The hottest property in the division, Ray Graydon, was also snapped up from Bristol Rovers.

As the season wore on the divisional title race became a formality, Villa eventually topping the table with a club record 70 points. Their average gate had been 31,952, more then the next two highest combined. A crowd of

Official Programme 10p

THE FOOTBALL LEAGUE

CUP FINAL

ASTON VILLA
VERSUS
TOTTENHAM HOTSPUR
Saturday, February 27th, 1971.
Kick-off 3.30 p.m.
EMPIRE STADIUM WEMBLEY

45,586 saw Villa bid farewell to Division Three, ironically against Chesterfield, the club against who the great adventure had begun. Villa also won the FA Youth Cup in 1972, beating Liverpool in the final, thanks in part to Brian Little and John Gidman. Two future England internationals in a Third Division youth team – only at Aston Villa.

While most supporters enjoyed the feeling of winning again after decades of decline and still regard the two seasons Villa spent in such lowly company with affection, more logical views were also heard. "The most humiliating two seasons in the club's history" was the verdict of local reporter Tom Duckworth, while director and former player Harry Parkes refused to join in the prolonged celebrations, saying: "It was like Muhammed Ali winning the Boys Brigade championship." And although they had been memorable years, Villa supporters were glad to see them come to an end – although the bank managers and accountants of the clubs they left behind weren't so happy.

Villa, being Villa, celebrated promotion in time-honoured fashion, with boardroom arguments, the brief overthrow of Doug Ellis and an extraordinary general meeting of shareholders which was held under floodlights on the Villa Park pitch. This resulted in the removal from the board of new chairman Jim Hartley during scenes of infighting which lasted until well into the new season. Only at the Villa…

THE STORY OF THE VILLA
UPS AND DOWNS
AND UPS AND...
1968-92

The new board was, in the main,

made up of young local businessmen, exactly the sort of modern thinkers needed to breathe life into the stagnating edifice of Villa Park. And they did it in style. Whatever Doug Ellis was later to become, his flair for publicity meant that the club was rarely out of the newspapers, and Tommy Docherty's eye for the quick quip helped immeasurably.

For the first time in years Villa fans felt the club was on the rise again and they responded; gates trebled almost overnight, a share issue raised over £200,000 and results improved as the relegation that seemed inevitable before Christmas was avoided with ease. Promotion back to the First Division seemed a formality; nothing could stop the Villa.

But despite spending big money on new players during the summer of 1969, results were poor and Docherty was sacked in January of the following year. His replacement, reserve team coach and former Villa player Vic Crowe, was unable to prevent the team from going down to the Third Division. Yet far from being a disaster, relegation was to prove the springboard from which Villa would reach the heights once more. In 1970/71 there was an epic League Cup semi-final win over Manchester United, followed by a narrow defeat in the final to Spurs. During the following season Villa were watched by record gates, spent a record amount of money for a Third Division side and romped away with the title, winning the FA Youth Cup as a bonus.

Tomy Docherty in 1969 with new signings (from left) Bruce Rioch, Chico Hamilton and Neil Rioch

Vic Crowe was unable to achieve another promotion and was sacked in 1974. His successor, Ron Saunders, was an instant success. With a side consisting almost entirely of players bought or nurtured by Crowe, Saunders won promotion to the First Division at the first attempt in fine style, as well as winning the League Cup with a 1-0 win over Norwich City. The star of the side was winger Ray Graydon, but also playing a big part was Brian Little, who at the end of the season became the first Villa player for many years to win an England cap.

Saunders then rebuilt the side and 1976/77 saw Villa finally back in the big time. The team, with a three-pronged attack of Little, Scottish star Andy Gray and local boy John Deehan leading the way, beat all-comers, including a 5-1 demolition of that season's European Cup winners Liverpool. They eventually finished fourth in the league, the club's highest place

since the thirties, and would have surely finished
higher had it not been for a backlog of fixtures
caused in part by a marathon League Cup run. Little
scored a hat-trick in the semi-final replay against
Queens Park Rangers at Highbury while a three-
game final versus Everton saw captain Chris Nicholl

Chris Nicholl flicks to
kick, Everton's Mike
Lyons doesn't know

scoring from 40 yards out and Little netting the winner in the dying moments of the second replay.

Several years then followed when injuries to key members of the team and boardroom upheavals – one of which led to Doug Ellis being removed from the board – saw disappointing league finishes. But Saunders was building his third successful side and 1980/81 saw Villa win their seventh title.

Captain Dennis Mortimer was an inspirational figure while the experienced Peter Withe, winger Tony Morley and Brummie forward Gary Shaw – the most promising young striker in the game – scored goals almost at will. The season was best summed up with Villa's 2-0 win over Liverpool at Villa Park, where Mortimer burst from midfield to score the team's second goal in a game which killed off the hopes of the reigning champions.

But being Villa, controversy was never far away and the club was rocked in February 1982 when Saunders walked out after a row with new chairman Ron Bendall, only to be installed as manager of Birmingham City the following week. He was replaced by his assistant, Tony Barton, under whose guidance the team went on to win that season's European Cup, beating Bayern Munich 1-0 in the final. Peter Withe scored the winning goal.

That triumph was followed up by Villa winning the European Super Cup in 1982/83, with a stormy second leg against Barcelona finishing 3-1 to Villa after three players were sent off and a host more

booked. Hopes were high for the following season but serious injuries to Gary Shaw and highly-rated midfielder Gordon Cowans led to the team finishing tenth in the league. Manager Barton was dismissed and replaced by Graham Turner of Second Division Shrewsbury Town. By now Doug Ellis had returned

Celebrating the 1981 title win in the dressing rooms at Highbury

as chairman and his cost-cutting measures led to
a slump in the team's fortunes, declining gates and
ultimately relegation to the Second Division in 1987.

However, Ellis produced a masterstroke when
unveiling Graham Taylor as the club's new
manager. Taylor had performed miracles in taking
unfashionable Watford from the Fourth Division to
runners-up in the first and did a similar job with
Villa. Promotion was achieved at the first attempt
and although the following season was disappointing,

David Platt rounds a
despairing Jim Leighton
in a 1989 league game
at Villa Park

1989/90 saw Villa finish runners-up. Star performers David Platt and Paul McGrath were bought for small fees in what were to prove two of the best transfer deals in the club's history.

Taylor took over the England manager's job after the 1990 World Cup and his replacement was the Czech national side's boss, Joszef Venglos. Villa were one of the first English sides to play in Europe again but, despite a memorable UEFA Cup win over Inter, the team lost 3-0 in the return leg and league form slumped, relegation only being avoided in the final week of the season.

Venglos had many revolutionary ideas, some of which are now regarded as commonplace in English football, but he had difficulty in being accepted at the time and was replaced as Villa manager by Ron Atkinson. The flamboyant Big Ron sold David Platt for £5.5 million to Italian side Bari and began buying players almost wholesale, such was the turnover of new arrivals at Villa Park.

Off the field there were great changes taking place in English football, with clubs in the First Division breaking away to form a new Premier League and satellite TV company Sky investing heavily to win the contract to show live games. It was, as Sky put it in their advertising, a whole new ball game.

ASTON VILLA
COMIC STRIP HISTORY
3

IN 1938 VILLA WERE ASKED TO PLAY IN A POST-SEASON TOUR OF GERMANY, THEN UNDER NAZI RULE... THEY WERE DUE TO PLAY A GERMAN REPRESENTATIVE ELEVEN...

THE FOREIGN OFFICE ARE ASKING US TO PERFORM A NAZI SALUTE BEFORE THE MATCH...

NOT LIKELY... NOT ME...

BECAUSE THEY REFUSED, THE GERMAN NEWSPAPERS CRITICISED THEM...

NOW THEY ARE **ORDERING** US TO DO IT BEFORE OUR NEXT MATCH!

THE VILLA TEAM RELUCTANTLY BEGAN THE HATED SALUTE, BUT RATHER THAN DOING IT PROPERLY, THE PLAYERS STARTED MAKING V SIGNS, OR WAVING...

NOT KNOWING WHAT THEY MEANT, THE CROWD ROARED THEIR APPROVAL.

TACTICS

VICTORIAN PIONEERS

George Ramsay introduced the concept of dribbling with the ball to the Villa and as the team became successful, the team's style of play was further refined to incorporate the passing style which better players were able to utilise.

The arrival of trainer Joe Grierson in 1893 saw the team moved up a further notch as Grierson, in conjunction with captain John Devey, worked on ways in which to counter the strengths of the opposition – the first time this concept had been employed.

By now teams were lining up in the 2-3-5 style that would last for many years. Villa were not only masters of the system, they also had players whose versatility meant they could perform in ways other clubs couldn't match. Centre forward John Campbell, for example, would drop into midfield in order to pick up the ball, at a time when his counterparts rarely left the opposition penalty area. Wingers Charlie Athersmith and John Cowan did far more than take the ball to the goal line and hit a cross in the direction of their forwards. The half back line played accurately out to the wings while full backs were encouraged to make shorter passes to their team-mates rather than hit hopeful balls upfield.

Villa carried all before them, using ideas and tactics that would not become commonplace until much later. The reason why the Villa style was not copied by other clubs was simple – no other club had players good enough. Not until Herbert Chapman arrived in the late 1920s to move football along once more would there be a team who came close to emulating Villa's domination of the game three decades earlier.

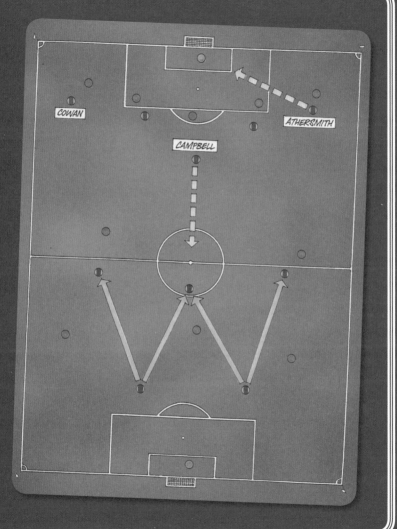

COWAN

ATHERSMITH

CAMPBELL

THE 110%ERS

Ron Saunders' teams were known for their teamwork, but to call them short of flair was unfair. The side which gained promotion had genuine wingers and goalscoring forwards, while the three-pronged attack which spearheaded the side of 1976/77 is still remembered with fondness. By 1980/81 Saunders had reverted to what would be seen now as a 4-4-2 system, which fitted the strengths of his side.

Two solid central defenders in Ken McNaught and Allan Evans combined with full backs who attacked. In midfield, the central duo of hard-running Dennis Mortimer and the ball-playing artist Gordon Cowans was complemented by Des Bremner playing wide right, where he was willing to cover for marauding full back Kenny Swain. And on the left wing was the mercurial, magnificent Tony Morley. Centre forward Peter Withe played alongside goal poacher extraordinaire Gary Shaw and Villa were a match for any other side in the country.

The opposition attack would be stopped in its tracks by Evans or McNaught, who would then hand the ball over to Mortimer, bursting unstoppably through the middle, or Cowans, whose precision ball out wide would find its man with unerring accuracy. Sometimes it would be Morley on the left wing who continued the attack. Sometimes it would be the overlapping Swain. A defender would be beaten, a pinpoint cross sent over to Withe, the archetypal target man who, if he didn't get an attempt on goal himself would either hold up the ball or head it down for the quicksilver Shaw. Given less than half a chance the ball was in the back of the net. It was simple, on its day it was unbeatable and it conquered Europe.

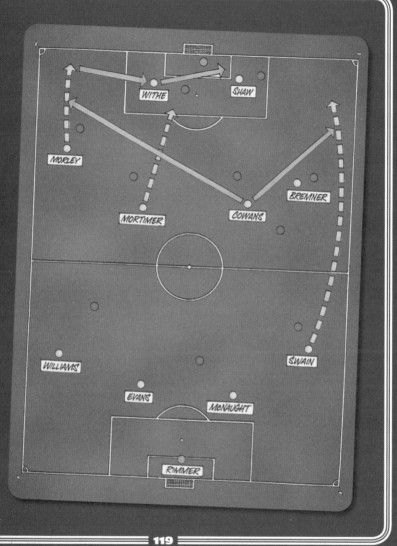

ONE MOMENT IN TIME

By the early nineties the 3-5-2 formation was starting to become fashionable, seen as a flexible way of providing strength both in attack and defence and providing an alternative to the 4-4-2 which had become predictable and easily countered. Villa had been using overlapping full backs for many years and Graham Taylor had introduced a three-man central defence so the idea was hardly revolutionary, but it took Brian Little's arrival to see this system used to its best effect.

The basis of 3-5-2 was that the full backs effectively became wingers, Alan Wright and Gary Charles fitting the bill perfectly. They also had three of the best central defenders in the country – Gareth Southgate, Ugo Ehiogu and Paul McGrath, who covered when their wing backs were attacking.

In midfield, Tommy Johnson originally played off the two strikers but when he lost his place in the side through injury, replacement Ian Taylor was a more box-to-box player, doing his share of defensive work as well as scoring vital goals. In 1995/96 Villa began to challenge the top sides and the system they played was part of their success. As Little said of his team, "It didn't play in straight lines, it had a lot of flair."

Unfortunately, the disadvantages of 3-5-2 were soon exposed. If the wide men were pushed back, midfield would be outnumbered and the forwards starved of service. The increasing pace of football also meant that wing backs were unable to cope with the amount of running they needed to do. For many managers who stuck to the system, five defenders and a defensive midfielder stifling creativity became the order of the day and soon 3-5-2 had been quietly forgotten.

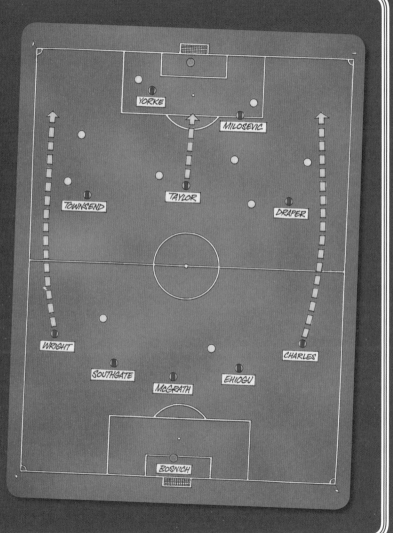

MARTIN O'NEILL'S CLARET AND BLUE ARMY

Under Martin O'Neill, Villa's play has been clearly identifiable. O'Neill's reliance on players from a traditionally English background has been criticised in some quarters, although it enables him to stamp his mark on both them and the team.

Villa's style of play is more direct than many teams – which has led to them being unfairly labelled a long-ball outfit, usually by managers whose teams they've just beaten.

What is undeniable is that O'Neill's side is one of the quickest in the Premier League. With players such as Gabriel Agbonlahor and Ashley Young in the team, Villa always have the option for the quick break out of defence. Indeed, their style is based on counter-attacking, with Villa particularly dangerous at set-pieces when central defenders can be used to good effect. It may sometimes be basic, but it plays to the strengths of the players Martin has at his disposal.

Like every Villa manager in the modern era, Martin has built his team around two dominant men at the back – the 2009/10 version being James Collins and Richard Dunne, with support from Carlos Cuellar. Stilyan Petrov shores up the midfield, James Milner supplies the central guile with Young and Stewart Downing on the wings. Up front are John Carew, on his day as good a target man as any in the game, and the lightening-quick Agbonlahor. Or sometimes it's a five-man midfield with just one striker and the wingers feeding off him.

Whatever the formation, it's a system which has made Villa one of the most difficult sides to beat in the Premier League and, particularly away from home, has brought some exciting results.

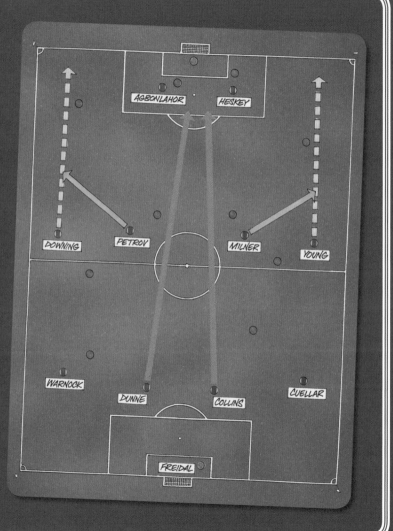

GREAT GAFFERS

The first man to be appointed Villa

manager was Jimmy McMullan in 1934. However, for many years the manager was still regarded as a junior figure at the club, subservient to the wishes of the board, and this only really changed with the arrival of Joe Mercer in 1958.

Mercer was in charge as Villa went down into the Second Division thanks to a last-minute defeat at the Hawthorns. But the team bounced back immediately, becoming Second Division champions the following season and were the inaugural winners of the League Cup in 1961.

The side of the time featured a host of highly promising young players, dubbed the Mercer Minors, and the future looked bright for both them and the club. However, injury to several key players led to a decline in the side's fortunes.

As a player, Jimmy McMullan captained Scotland's famous Wembley wizards

Ron Saunders raises the 1975 League Cup, watched by captain Ian Ross

FA Cup defeat at the hands of Fourth Division Aldershot in January 1964 intensified the pressure on Mercer and at the end of that season the manager was taken ill, after suffering what was later revealed to be a stroke, and sacked during the summer. His subsequent success with Manchester City, which came during the lowest point in Villa's history, showed the short-sighted nature of that decision.

While Villa went through a succession of managers in an attempt to get back to the top flight, it took the most successful boss in the club's history to finally get them there. Ron Saunders was appointed as a successor to the highly-rated Vic Crowe in 1974, winning promotion at the first attempt and with the added bonus of the League Cup in 1975, Villa's first trophy for 18 years.

Saunders then put together what is often referred

to as the most attractive Villa side of the post-war era, the team which in 1976/77 finished fourth in the league and won the League Cup once more. With Andy Gray and Brian Little spearheading the attack Villa were at times unstoppable, their dazzling performances reaching a climax with a 5-1 destruction of Liverpool.

The next three years were ones of anti-climax as injuries and boardroom infighting overshadowed Saunders' rebuilding plans, but 1980/81 saw his third team unveiled to the world. Built around the manager's traditional ethos of team work (his programme notes always called for 110% effort) and with Tony Morley and Gary Shaw providing

Ron Atkinson brought champagne football to Villa in the 1990s

the flair, Villa battled for the league title with Ipswich Town. They eventually raced ahead as the East Anglian media favourites cracked during the final weeks of the season. Villa's first league title for 71 years was finally secured with a four point margin.

Saunders was always his own man, unwilling to court favour with the press and willing to upset players with whom he had fallen out, as witnessed by the way in which he got rid of John Gidman and Andy Gray in 1979. This might have made him unpopular with sections of the wider footballing world but this 'us against the world' mentality, later perfected by Alex Ferguson, only made Villa supporters love him even more. He made it clear that he did everything for the fans, who in return held him in greater esteem than they had any other Villa boss before or since. Even his departure to Birmingham City in February 1982, amidst circumstances that have never been fully explained, was regarded as a temporary aberration and although he was an exile from Villa Park for many years, Saunders' recent match day appearances have seen the most successful manager in the club's history receive the acclaim he deserves.

Graham Taylor reversed years of decline

Ron Saunders' departure was followed by years of decline, reversed only by Graham Taylor, who found what he described as a "shambles" following relegation in 1987. Taylor left three years later to become manager of England with the club having just finished runners-up in the First Division. Taylor's team selections may have been unorthodox at times but they were effective. He also signed arguably the three greatest Villa players of the modern era in David Platt, Paul McGrath and Dwight Yorke, all of them bought at bargain prices.

Taylor was unable to bring any silverware to Villa Park but he rebuilt the club from top to bottom and left them in a fit state to face the challenges of the way the game was evolving.

The next big name Villa manager was the biggest name of the lot – Ron Atkinson. With a champagne image (even if the reality was quiet different) and football to match Ron courted the limelight and as one sage put it, "When Ron was around Villa got the publicity they deserved." After a season of frantic rebuilding with around two dozen players either coming or going, Atkinson took Villa to the top of the Premier League in 1992/93 on a tidal wave of scintillating football, during which time they made the Goal of the Month competition almost an in-house tournament. Villa were unable to maintain this form until the end of the season, fading to finish runners-up to Manchester United, but the following year saw Ron's finest tactical hour as his side outfought the Old Trafford side to win a memorable League Cup final.

Villa's next manager, former playing hero Brian Little, rebuilt the side with

Brian Little built a credible challenge for the top

Martin O'Neill arrived with a reputation as one of the best coaches in the country

Dwight Yorke up front and a 3-5-2 formation used to good effect. Little's team finished fourth in 1995/96, winning the League Cup once more with a one-sided demolition of Leeds. They were seen by many as the team most likely to challenge Manchester United but a series of unwise buys, including the fateful purchase of Stan Collymore, upset the balance of the team and Little departed in 1998.

Several managers later and the summer of 2006 saw the arrival at Villa Park of not only a new owner in Randy Lerner but also of Martin O'Neill, one of the most highly-rated managers in the country. The past four years have seen O'Neill assemble a team with a core of young English-based players, although he has been criticised for a safety-first buying policy and uninspiring tactics. Three consecutive top-six finishes would indicate that O'Neill has, at least, built the foundations for future success.

MEMORABLE
MATCHES

VILLA 4 MAN UNITED 6

FA Cup third round, Villa Park, 10th January 1948

It may seem strange to include in a series of great games a seemingly ordinary cup tie in which Villa lost. But no other game ever played at Villa Park has been regarded by so many of those who saw it as the greatest they ever witnessed.

Trevor Ford almost levelled the score at 5-5

A hint of what was to come took place when the Villa sped downfield straight from the kick-off and went a goal up thanks to George Edwards after 13½ seconds. Any thoughts that this would be an easy victory were soon dispelled though, as United equalised six minutes later and went in at half time 5-1 up.

But Villa summoned the old Astonian cup-fighting spirit and scored soon after the re-start when United goalkeeper George Crompton failed to hold a corner from Edwards. On a typically heavy Villa Park pitch the team gave up trying to match the skilful artistry of their opponents and began to put their own superior strength to good use with long balls aimed beyond the visiting defenders.

With 70 minutes gone a free kick from Dickie Dorsett was rammed home by Leslie Smith. 5-3. The crowd was now at fever pitch and the Villa Roar was cranked up even higher when, with nine minutes remaining, Dorsett's penalty made the score 5-4.

The Manchester United team that went on to beat Blackpool in the final

With the crowd roaring them on, Villa's aerial bombardment continued to trouble the United defence. Hearts stopped when Trevor Ford hit the bar with a minute remaining. Almost immediately United broke away, forced a corner and the ball was bundled home to make the game safe. The Villa players trudged from the field, hardly able to summon the strength to get back to the dressing room such had been the extent of their efforts.

The crowd roared their appreciation of both teams, but the finest tribute was later paid by journalist Geoffrey Green who had covered the match for *The Times*. Whenever he was asked the best game he saw during his long career, the veteran scribe would always reply, without hesitation, "Aston Villa versus Manchester United in the 1948 FA Cup third round."

Villa: Jones, Potts, Parkes, Dorsett, Moss (F), Lower (E), Edwards, Martin, Ford, Brown, Smith

Scorers: Edwards (2), Smith, Dorsett

Attendance: 58,683

VILLA 5 LIVERPOOL 1

Division One, Villa Park, 15th December 1976

If the 1948 cup tie with Manchester United was the greatest match seen at Villa Park, this was surely the best performance the ground has ever witnessed.

Liverpool were reigning league champions and destined to win the European Cup a few months later, but they were ripped apart by a Villa side in which every player was at the peak of his game.

John Deehan netted twice

The fun started after nine minutes when John Robson's cross was met by Andy Gray, who headed past Clemence to put Villa one up. Three minutes later Dennis Mortimer burst through from midfield to lay on a chance for John Deehan, who slid the ball under Clemence.

On 20 minutes a shot from Gray was deflected into the path of Deehan, whose shot beat Clemence at the near post.

Villa supporters were already in a state of delirium but more was to come after half an hour when John Gidman's run along the wing led to the ball being played to Brian Little, whose curling shot from 15 yards out notched the best goal of the night.

Liverpool did eventually start playing and pulled a goal back after 40 minutes, when Ray Kennedy's shot inside a crowded penalty area beat unsighted keeper Jake Findlay. Villa's response came a minute before half time, when Dennis Mortimer's corner was headed home by Andy Gray. Clemence was again left stranded and wondering just what was going on. After all, any sort of defeat was rare for Liverpool, much less one in which they were five goals down at half time.

The second half was an anti-climax, but no matter. The game remains Liverpool's heaviest defeat for almost half a century and the headline in the following day's *Liverpool Echo* summed the night up. It read "Devastation. Pure and simple."

As an aside, if anyone felt worse than Ray Clemence it was ATV Head of Sport Gary Newbon who, with broadcast regulations allowing just one game to be recorded from that night's league programme, chose to cover events at the Baseball Ground, where Derby County's new signing Derek Hales was making his debut. That one finished 0-0.

Villa: Findlay, Gidman, Robson, Phillips, Young, Mortimer, Deehan, Little, Gray, Cropley, Carrodus

Scorers: Gray (2), Deehan (2), Little

Attendance: 42,821

VILLA 3 MAN UNITED 1

Coca-Cola Cup final, Wembley Stadium, 27th March 1994

The best team may always win the league but in a one-off game tactics and sheer will to win can often triumph. Never was this shown better than at Wembley in Ron Atkinson's finest hour.

Villa had lost their previous three league games while the free-scoring United were on course for a record-breaking domestic treble. But manager Atkinson had an idea of how to stop them. He'd been analysing on their televised game with Arsenal a few days earlier and saw United's wide men had been nullified by Arsenal using five midfielders. Big Ron thought Villa could do a similar job. "We didn't have anyone who could go man to man with them, so I thought we could take them with numbers," he later explained.

With Tony Daley and Dalian Atkinson tying up the United wing threat and Dean Saunders as a lone striker, there was a surprise call-up for 19-year-old Graham Fenton whose previous experience amounted to a handful of first-team appearances and a

Coca Cola Cup
Final

ASTON VILLA F.C.
V
MANCHESTER UNITED F.C.
27th March 1994
Wembley

loan spell with West Brom. Fenton never did have the glittering career that was predicted for him, but for one afternoon he was a big star. So were the rest of the team.

Atkinson's tactics worked perfectly. United's wide players were too busy coping with the threat posed by Atkinson and Daley to get forward. Fenton totally outshone Eric Cantona, pushing him ever deeper and out of harm's way. Saunders, meanwhile, was doing the work of two men. No forward ever covered so much ground or chased so many seemingly lost causes as Villa's Welsh international did that day.

Villa went a goal up after 25 minutes when Saunders laid a ball on for Dalian Atkinson, who slotted home with his usual precision. On 75 minutes the advantage was doubled when Kevin Richardson's shot was diverted in by Saunders.

Mark Hughes pulled a goal back with eight minutes remaining, but in injury time a shot from Atkinson was handled on the line by Andrei Kanchelskis. The United winger was sent off, Saunders converted the penalty and Villa's first trophy for 12 years was won.

Villa: Bosnich, Barrett, Staunton, McGrath, Teale, Daley, Fenton, Richardson, Townsend, Atkinson Saunders

Scorers: Atkinson, Saunders (2)

Attendance: 77,231

VILLA 6 BLACKBURN ROVERS 4

Carling Cup semi final second leg, Villa Park, 20th January 2010

Already a goal up from the first leg at Ewood Park, this should have been a straightforward progression to Villa's first final appearance in ten years. But Villa don't do things the easy way.

Nikola Kalinic levelled the aggregate scores after ten minutes. After 26, he'd put Blackburn into the lead and the 'straightforward' tie was looking anything but. Blackburn could have gone further ahead, but with Villa's first real attack Stephen Warnock pulled a goal back on half an hour, to the chagrin of the Blackburn players who felt there had been a foul in the build-up to Warnock's strike.

They were even more aggrieved ten minutes later when Christopher Samba was sent off after committing a foul inside the penalty area, giving James Milner the chance to put Villa 3-2 ahead in the tie from the resultant spot-kick.

Half time came with Villa in the ascendancy, a goal up and with their demoralised opponents down to ten men. They were soon even more hopeful, as an own goal was followed by Gabriel Agbonlahor and Emile Heskey putting Villa further ahead. Surely nothing could possibly go wrong now. No team on earth could throw away a four goal lead at home to a team who had had a player sent off.

Villa couldn't, but they did their best. Within seconds of Heskey's goal Blackburn pulled one back, courtesy of Martin Olsson. Brett Emerton made the score 5-4 on the night and another Blackburn goal could have made the last few minutes interesting ones. But the expected onslaught didn't happen and deep into injury time Ashley Young made doubly certain of the tie as well as giving Villa Park its first double-figure scoreline for almost 50 years.

At the final whistle the crowd seemed unsure whether to laugh in disbelief or cheer with joy. The game was never nail-biting enough to be a truly great one; from the minute Villa scored their first goal they were in charge and the result was in no real doubt well before half time. But for sheer incredulity it will live on in the memory.

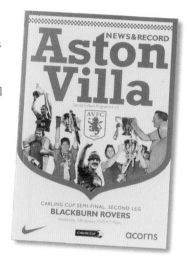

Villa: Guzan, Cuellar, Dunne, Collins, Warnock, Young, Milner, Petrov, Downing, Agbonlahor, Heskey

Scorers: Warnock, Milner, Nzongi (og), Agbonlahor, Heskey, Young

Attendance: 40,406

ASTON VILLA
COMIC STRIP HISTORY
4

ONE EVENING IN 1924 VILLA PLAYER THOMAS BALL AND HIS WIFE RETURNED FROM A LOCAL PUB TO FIND THEIR NEIGHBOUR, GEORGE STAGG, AWAITING THEM...

YOU SHOULD SEE THE MESS YOUR DOG HAS MADE OF MY GARDEN. I'M **VERY** ANGRY...

MY DOG WOULDN'T DO THAT...

AS THE ARGUMENT RAGED STAGG, A FIRST WORLD WAR VETERAN, PRODUCED HIS SERVICE REVOLVER.

TAKE THAT!

THOMAS DIED ALMOST INSTANTLY, THE ONLY ENGLISH PROFESSIONAL FOOTBALLER EVER TO BE MURDERED.

STAGG WAS CHARGED WITH MURDER AND SENTENCED TO DEATH, ALTHOUGH HE WAS LATER REPRIEVED AND RELEASED FROM PRISON IN 1945...

...HUNG BY THE NECK UNTIL DEAD...

THE STORY OF THE VILLA
A WHOLE NEW
BALL GAME
1992-2010

The Premier League began

began in 1992/93 and Villa came close to becoming its first champions. Dean Saunders and Dalian Atkinson were in irresistible form and the sublime quality of the team's football reminded supporters of the side that had won the League Cup back in 1977.

Atkinson won the Goal of the Season award for a magnificent effort away at Wimbledon but the team unfortunately ran out of steam, eventually finishing runners-up to Manchester United. They may not have won the title but they did provide supporters with a host of memories.

League form was mixed in 1993/94, but a

Dalian Atkinson scores in the 1994 Coca-Cola Cup final win over Manchester United...

pulsating League Cup run climaxed as Villa got a
modicum of revenge by beating United 3-1 in the
final. However, the following season got off to a poor
start and Atkinson was sacked in November 1994,
replaced by former playing favourite Brian Little,
then manager of Leicester City. Little kept Villa safe
from relegation and turned the team's fortunes round
dramatically in 1995/96.

Expected to struggle once more, they began the
season with a stunning 3-1 victory at home to
Manchester United, eventually finishing fourth in the
table and winning the League Cup for the fifth time
in the club's history, beating Leeds 3-0 in a one-sided
final. Star of the side was Dwight Yorke, bought for a

...and there was
another win in the
same competition
in 1996

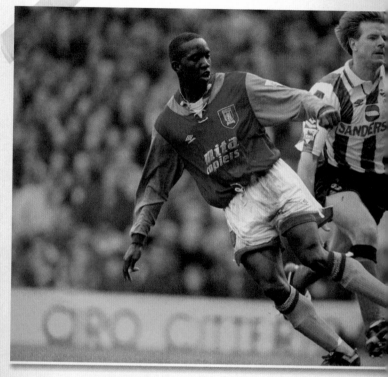

Dwight Yorke
blossomed under
Brian Little

small fee by Graham Taylor, often overlooked by Ron
Atkinson and now a world-class striker under Little.
Villa finished fifth in 1996/97 and with record
signing Stan Collymore, a £7 million buy from
Liverpool in the summer of 1997, hopes were high
that the team would once more challenge for the title.
Unfortunately Collymore would have a disastrous

effect on the team's morale and as the season went from bad to worse, Little resigned. He was surprisingly replaced by his former coach John Gregory, who had earlier left Villa to manage Wycombe Wanderers.

Gregory proved immediately beneficial to the team's fortunes, winning them a place in the UEFA Cup once more and starting 1998/99 with a club record run of form. The side fell away badly in the second half of the season and began 1999/2000 in a similar vein, although they later recovered and reached the FA Cup final for the first time in almost half a century of trying.

Defeat by Chelsea in this game was the signal for two more years of acrimony in which Gregory's negative tactics were often criticised by many supporters and the manager openly fell out with Doug Ellis on a regular basis. Gregory spent heavily, and although much of this outlay was recouped by sales, such as the £12.6 million received from Manchester United for Dwight Yorke, his record in the transfer market was poor.

Villa settled into a best-of-the-rest position where every season seemed to feature a good run followed by a bad one and supporters grew increasingly dissatisfied with the way the club was being run. The mood of the time was not improved by the safety-first tactics employed by the manager, whose main priority seemed to be avoiding giving Ellis an excuse to sack him. The inevitable parting of the ways came with Gregory's resignation in February 2002 and his replacement by Graham Taylor, who had been serving as a Villa director since stepping down from the Watford job some months previously.

Taylor's return was not a happy one. The game had changed since his glory days at Villa Park over a decade earlier, there was little money to spend on new players and the club was split, with fans, players and management at loggerheads with each other. After another season struggling against relegation Taylor resigned and was replaced by David O'Leary.

O'Leary got off to a good start, the team finishing sixth in 2003/04 and narrowly missing out on European qualification. This, though, was as good as it got, and by 2005/06 the situation was becoming critical. There was yet another battle against relegation and an embarrassing League Cup exit at the hands of Doncaster Rovers.

Supporters were regularly protesting against the now-octogenarian Doug Ellis, although such was O'Leary's unpopularity after several remarks about the fans that it was reckoned his greatest achievement at Villa Park was to become even more disliked than the chairman.

The end for O'Leary came during the summer of

2006, following a bizarre sequence of events in which several players were reported to have sent a letter to a local newspaper criticising the way the club was being run. Although there was no direct evidence to link O'Leary to the letter, he was forced to leave the club, to a general feeling of relief from all concerned.

For some reason known only to himself, O'Leary seemed to have gone out of his way to alienate

Elation at the 2000 FA Cup semi-final penalty shoot out win over Bolton Wanderers

The good times
are rolling again
for Villa fans

everyone – press, supporters, players and finally
the chairman.

While fans were trying to understand this
particular story, the news broke that American
billionaire Randy Lerner was interested in buying
the Villa. As if this wasn't good enough, O'Leary's
replacement was rumoured to be Martin O'Neill,

looking for a way back into football after leaving Celtic a year earlier to nurse his seriously-ill wife. O'Neill was appointed, Lerner took over and once more everything in the claret and blue garden seemed rosy.

Under Lerner's ownership the club has been financially secure and investment forthcoming not only on players, but also on the Bodymoor Heath training ground and in areas such as the Holte Hotel and renovating the ground.

The last few seasons have been ones of quiet progress. The team has regularly finished in the top six, European qualification attained (although O'Neill seems to regard getting there as more important than actually playing in what is now the Europa League and has often fielded weakened sides in the tournament), and quality players such as Ashley Young and James Milner signed. There was a return to Wembley for the 2010 League Cup final, although this ended in a 2-1 defeat at the hands of Manchester United.

After the inconsistencies of the past few decades, Villa supporters can be satisfied with the current state of affairs.

GREAT SCOTS

Aston Villa were an ordinary team kicking a ball around on Aston Park before a young Scot named George Ramsay begged a game with them and proceeded to revolutionise world football. Not only did this émigré from north of the border show the Villa how to play the game properly, he also began a tradition of Scotsmen at Villa Park which has continued throughout the years.

Victorian Birmingham, the 'city of a thousand trades' was expanding rapidly and needed a constantly-increasing source of labour to maintain its role as the workshop of the world. Men arrived from all over the country to work in the city and naturally enough they also sought somewhere to spend their leisure hours.

One such arrival was Archie Hunter, a talented footballer who originally wanted to sign for Calthorpe. But he couldn't find their ground in Edgbaston and upon hearing that his fellow Scot Ramsay was Villa captain, joined them instead. Hunter went on to succeed Ramsay as skipper and became the first great Villa player, leading

the side which began Villa's glory years by winning the FA Cup of 1887. Another Scot, William McGregor, also became involved with the club at around this time. Although he was no player, McGregor was the great visionary who founded the Football League and who, along with Ramsay, helped Villa to be run in such a way that they soon became the most powerful club in the world. It was also McGregor who, reputedly, introduced the Scottish lion rampant badge to the club.

The Villa double-winning side of 1897 featured Caledonian brothers James and John Cowan (the former once going missing so as to win the Powderhall Sprint back in his native land) as well as John Campbell, who is believed to be the first man to win both the FA Cup and league championship in England and Scotland.

In the immediate post-war period Dr Victor Milne came down from Edinburgh to practice medicine in Birmingham and found himself one of the last amateurs to

George Ramsay (third row from the front, on the left) can be seen behind the visionary William McGregor (bearded) with an early Villa side

play for Villa, appearing at centre half in the 1924 FA Cup final. The following decade saw Jimmy Gibson move from Partick Thistle to become a part of Villa's most famous half back line.

Villa's first manager was a Scotsman, Jimmy McMullen, as was Villa's first post-war boss, former team captain Alex Massie. In 1968 the consortium led by Doug Ellis that took over the club immediately installed Scotsman Tommy Docherty as manager. Docherty's time at Villa Park may not have been long but it was vital in kickstarting the club's revival. He also signed Bruce Rioch, who although born in England later went on to captain Scotland by virtue of his father's birthplace. And of course at this time Charlie Aitken, who would surely have become another of Villa's Scottish internationals had he been playing in any other era, was on his way to becoming the club's record appearance maker.

Ron Saunders may have been uncompromisingly English, but he knew the benefits of having a strong tartan influence in his side. Saunders' first captain was Glaswegian defender Ian Ross, who led the Villa to promotion and became only the second Villa skipper to lift a trophy at Wembley, in his case the League Cup in 1975. Saunders then signed Andy Gray from Dundee United and the player was instrumental in Villa's success during 1976/77, as was midfielder Alex Cropley, the epitome of that breed of Scottish midfielder who were as ferocious in winning the ball as they were artistic in its distribution.

Saunders then had the Scottish central defensive pairing of Ken McNaught and Allan Evans as the rock on which the 1980/81 title-winning side was built, also including midfielder Des Bremner as a vital component of that memorable team. The Scottish national side of the period must have been well blessed for these three to have been ignored so often.

Villa then unfortunately appointed former Celtic captain Billy McNeill as manager, although the less said about that particular decision the better. Fortunately Graham Taylor was soon on hand, ably assisted first by now-veteran club captain Allan Evans and another former Celt, Alan McInally. Evans then returned to Villa Park in the 1990s as assistant manager to Brian Little and helped oversee the winning of Villa's latest trophy, the League Cup in 1996.

This is, of course, how Andy Gray always dressed away from the football pitch

There is also a link to Scotland in the Villa set-up today, albeit a tenuous one, in that Martin O'Neill's previous job before joining the club was at Celtic.

There are few top-class Scots footballers nowadays, which is a source of great pity to everyone who appreciates the enormous influence Scotsmen have had on the game. And for the Villa such a deficiency is doubly disappointing. After all, we've relied on them more than most. The very fabric of Aston Villa FC definitely includes an element of tartan.

HONOURS AND RECORDS

MAJOR HONOURS
WINNERS
European Cup 1982
Football League 1894, 1896, 1897, 1899, 1900, 1910, 1981
FA Cup 1887, 1895, 1897, 1905, 1913, 1920, 1957
Football League Cup 1961, 1975, 1977, 1994, 1996
European Super Cup 1983

Charity Shield winners 1981 (shared)
Football League Division Two 1938, 1959
Football League Division Three 1972
Intertoto Cup 2001
FA Youth Cup 1972, 1980, 2002
Premier Reserve League North 2004

Premier Reserve League South
2008, 2009, 2010
Central League 1930, 1964, 1993

RUNNERS-UP
Football League 1904, 1921, 1977
FA Cup 1926, 1933, 1955, 1981
League Cup 1974

INDIVIDUAL HONOURS
PFA PLAYER OF THE YEAR
Andy Gray 1977
David Platt 1990
Paul McGrath 1993

PFA YOUNG PLAYER OF THE YEAR
Andy Gray 1977
Gary Shaw 1981
Ashley Young 2009
James Milner 2010

MANAGER OF THE YEAR
Ron Saunders 1975, 1981

CLUB RECORDS
Most points in a season (calculated as three for a win): 102, 1971/72
Most league wins in a season: 32, 1971/72
Most league goals in a season: 128, 1930/31
Fewest league goals conceded: 32,
1971/72 (46 games) and 1974/75 (42 games)
Consecutive league wins: 9, 1910/11
Consecutive league games unbeaten: 15, 1910/11
Record win: 13-0 v Wednesbury Old Athletic, FA Cup first round, 3rd October 1886
Record league win: 12-2 v Accrington Stanley, Division One, 12th March 1892
Record League Cup win: 8-1 v Exeter City, second round, 9th October 1985
Record European win: 5-0 v Valur, 16th September 1981
Record defeat: 8-1 v Blackburn Rovers, FA Cup third round, 2nd March 1889
Record attendance: 76,588 v Derby County, FA Cup sixth round, 2nd March, 1946
Record league attendance: 69,492 v Wolves, Division One, 27th December 1949
Record League Cup attendance, 62,500 v Manchester United, 23rd December 1970
Highest average league attendance: 47,320, 1948/49
Lowest attendance at Villa Park: 2,900 v Bradford City, Divison One, 13th February 1951

Lowest FA Cup attendance at Villa Park: 12,205 v Millwall, 25th January 1986

Lowest League Cup attendance at Villa Park: 7,678 v Exeter City, 9th October 1985

Most appearances: Charlie Aitken, 660, 1961-76

Most league appearances: Charlie Aitken, 561, 1961-76

Most FA Cup appearances: Billy Walker, 53, 1920-33

Youngest player: Jimmy Brown, 15 years 349 days v Bolton, 17th September 1969

Oldest player: Ernest 'Mush' Callaghan, 39 years 257 days v Grimsby, 12th April 1947

Oldest debutant: Peter Schmeichel, 37 years 277 days v Spurs, 18th August 2001

Most capped player: Steve Staunton (right) – 64, Republic of Ireland

Most capped England player: Gareth Southgate, 42

Top goalscorer: Billy Walker, 244, 1919-33

Top league goalscorer: Harry Hampton, 215 in 11 seasons between 1904-1915

Most individual goals in a season: Thomas 'Pongo' Waring, 50, 1930/31

MISCELLANEOUS

- At one time or another Villa have held attendance records for the Football League, Premier League, Division One, Division Two, Division Three and the Central League.
- **Joszef Venglos was the first foreigner to be appointed manager of a top-flight English club.**
- Villa Park was one of three club grounds to host games in both the 1966 World Cup finals and Euro 96, the others being Old Trafford and Hillsborough.
- **Villa's 1994 League Cup final win over Manchester United was the last game to be covered by BBC Radio Five. At midnight on the day of the game the station changed its name to Five Live.**
- In 2008/09 Ashley Young became the first man to win three Premier League Player of the Month awards.
- **Villa Park has been used as the venue for 55 FA Cup semi finals, more than any other ground.**
- Villa's most successful player is Howard Spencer, who won five league championships and three FA Cups during his career with the club.

- **The most-played competitive fixture in English football is Aston Villa v Everton (or Everton v Aston Villa).**
- Villa full back Peter Aldis created a record on 1st September 1952 when he scored with a header against Sunderland from 35 yards.
- **Against Norwich City on 26th March 1980, Villa substitute Robert Hopkins scored with his only touch of the game.**
- Villa were the first club in Britain to donate their shirt sponsorship to a charity, children's hospice Acorns.
- **Villa Park hosted the last-ever Cup-Winners' Cup final, when Lazio beat Real Mallorca in 1999.**
- Villa are one of only three clubs, along with Blackburn Rovers and Everton, to have been founder members of both the Football League and the Premier League.
- **69 Villa players have become England internationals, more than at any other club.**
- Villa half back Thomas Ball is the only English professional footballer to have been murdered.
- **Former Villa goalkeeper John Burridge played for a record 15 Football League clubs.**
- Villa Park was the first English club ground to stage international football in three different centuries.